cronin

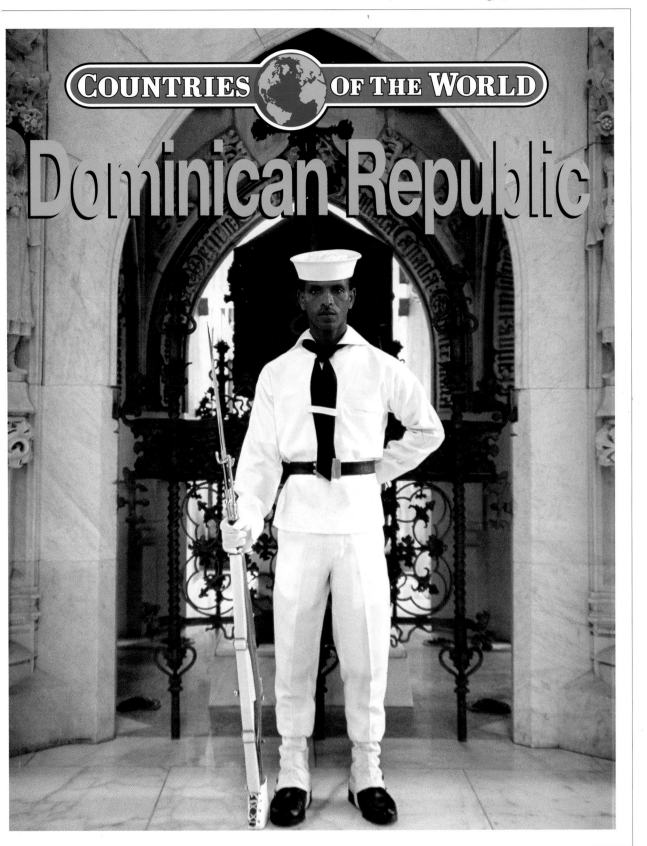

COUNTRIES OF THE WORLD

Dominican Republic

Gareth Stevens Publishing
A WORLD ALMANAC EDUCATION GROUP COMPANY

About the Authors: Kerry-Ann Morris is a historian, teacher, and freelance writer. She is pursuing a master of philosophy in history at the University of the West Indies in Jamaica. Nafisah Ismail obtained a bachelor of arts in mass communication from the Royal Melbourne Institute of Technology in Australia and is working as an editor in Singapore.

PICTURE CREDITS

AFP: 49, 72, 77, 78, 80, 81, 82, 85
ANA Press Agency: 5, 16, 34, 67
Art Directors & TRIP Photo Library: 47, 64, 89
Bes Stock Photo Library: cover, 37
Bettmann/Corbis: 15 (bottom), 38, 51, 76, 79
Steve Bly/Houserstock: 2, 26
Camera Press: 12 (top)
Focus Team — Italy: 3 (center) 18, 40, 41, 60, 62, 63
Chip & Rosa Maria de la Cueva Peterson: 6, 12 (bottom), 25, 39, 46
Paul Gerace: 51 (bottom)
The Hutchison Picture Library: 42, 87
International Photobank: 3 (top), 19, 32, 43, 75
IPS: 15 (top), 29, 56
Earl Kowall: 1, 3 (bottom), 4, 7, 17, 22, 24, 28, 33, 35, 36, 48, 53, 54, 55, 58, 59, 68, 74, 91
Lonely Planet Images: 20, 50, 57, 61, 69
Minerva Bernardino Foundation: 15 (center)
North Wind Picture Archives: 10, 66, 70
David Simson: 21, 23, 65
Times Editions: 27, 44, 52
Topham Picturepoint: 11, 13, 14 (both), 45, 73, 83, 84
Mireille Vautier: 8, 9, 30, 31

Digital Scanning by Superskill Graphics Pte Ltd

Written by
KERRY-ANN MORRIS
NAFISAH ISMAIL

Edited by
NAFISAH ISMAIL

Edited in the U.S. by
MONICA RAUSCH

Designed by
BENSON TAN

Picture research by
SUSAN JANE MANUEL
THOMAS KHOO

First published in North America in 2004 by
Gareth Stevens Publishing
A World Almanac Education Group Company
330 West Olive Street, Suite 100
Milwaukee, Wisconsin 53212 USA

Please visit our web site at
www.garethstevens.com
For a free color catalog describing
Gareth Stevens Publishing's list of
high-quality books and multimedia programs,
call 1-800-542-2595 (USA) or 1-800-387-3178 (Canada).
Gareth Stevens Publishing's Fax: (414) 332-3567.

© TIMES MEDIA PRIVATE LIMITED 2004
Originated and designed by
Times Editions
An imprint of Times Media Private Limited
A member of the Times Publishing Group
Times Centre, 1 New Industrial Road
Singapore 536196
http://www.timesone.com.sg/te

Library of Congress Cataloging-in-Publication Data
Morris, Kerry-Ann.
Dominican Republic / by Kerry-Ann Morris and Nafisah Ismail.
p. cm. — (Countries of the world)
Includes bibliographic references and index.
Summary: An introduction to the geography, history, government, lifestyles, culture, and current issues of the Dominican Republic.
ISBN 0-8368-3110-1 (lib. bdg.)
1. Dominican Republic—Juvenile literature. [1. Dominican Republic.]
I. Ismail, Nafisah. II. Title. III. Countries of the world (Milwaukee, Wis.)
F1934.2.M67   2004
972.93—dc22   2003060806

Printed in Singapore

1 2 3 4 5 6 7 8 9 08 07 06 05 04

Contents

AN OVERVIEW OF THE DOMINICAN REPUBLIC

The native Taino people used to call the Hispaniolan island "Quisqueya," or "Mother of All Lands."
The Dominican Republic is located in the center of the Caribbean region. The Caribbean Sea runs along the country's southern coast and the Atlantic Ocean along the northern coast. In the fifteenth century, the country was the starting point of European expansion into the rest of the Caribbean and the Americas. After much political conflict in its early history, the Dominican Republic seems set on a path toward greater stability and is making its mark on the international community.

Opposite: **Standing in the Santo Domingo harbor is a 150-foot (46-meter) statue of Fray Antón de Montesinos. The priest protested Spanish abuse of the Taino people in the sixteenth century.**

Below: **Musicians play at a restaurant in Santo Domingo.**

THE FLAG OF THE DOMINICAN REPUBLIC

The Dominican flag was first raised on February 27, 1844, to celebrate the country's independence. The flag features three colors — white, blue, and red. White symbolizes peace and unity for all Dominicans, while blue stands for the country's hopes for progress and freedom. Red represents the blood the country's heroes shed to liberate the nation. The flag has a white cross in the center that symbolizes the country's fight for freedom. At the center of the cross is the nation's shield of arms. The shield consists of a gold cross, four flags, and a Bible surrounded by palm and laurel branches.

Geography

The Dominican Republic has a total land area of 18,810 square miles (48,730 square kilometers). The country occupies the eastern two-thirds of the island of Hispaniola and shares the island with Haiti. The two countries are separated by a border stretching some 224 miles (360 kilometers). Santo Domingo is the capital city of the country and the oldest and second-largest city in the Caribbean. The city has a land area of 89 square miles (230 square km) and a population of about 3.5 million people.

Mountains and Valleys

The *cordillera* (kohr-dee-YEH-rah), or mountain chains, and valleys of the Dominican Republic separate the country into three regions. The Cordillera Septentrional is located in the northern region, while Cordillera Central is in the central region. Two mountain chains, Sierra de Neiba and Sierra de Bahoruco, are in the southwestern region. The Cordillera

NATIONAL PARKS

The Dominican Republic has a number of parks and reserves throughout the country, including the Jaragua, Isla Cabritos, Armando Bermúdez, and José del Carmen Ramírez national parks.
(A Closer Look, page 64)

Below: The Cibao Valley in the northern region of the Dominican Republic covers an area of 145 miles (233 km).

Central is the largest of the nation's mountain chains and contains the highest mountains, including the country's highest peak, Pico Duarte, at 10,417 feet (3,175 m).

Cibao Valley in the northern region is a very fertile area. Dominicans have used the valley for centuries for cattle ranching, rum production, and tobacco farming. Today, the Cibao Valley is still the most fertile area in the country and continues to be the main supplier of agricultural products.

Rivers

The Dominican Republic's two major rivers are the Yaque del Norte and the Yaque del Sur. The Yaque del Norte runs northwestward through the country's mountainous areas and jungles. The river measures some 184 miles (296 km) in length and is the longest river in the Dominican Republic. The river's basin area covers 2,719 square miles (7,044 square km).

The Yaque del Sur runs through the nation's southwestern region. The river is 114 miles (183 km) long and has a basin area of 1,919 square miles (4,972 square km).

Above: **The seven major drainage basins of the Dominican Republic are drained by several rivers and their tributaries.**

SEA CREATURES

The Dominican Republic's major rivers flow into the Atlantic Ocean and the Caribbean Sea. Whales, manatees, and endangered turtles are among the sea creatures that live in these bodies of water.
(A Closer Look, page 68)

Climate

The Dominican Republic is a tropical country with an annual average temperature of 78° Fahrenheit (26° Celsius). Differences in temperature between the summer and winter are very slight in most regions. In mountainous areas, however, the temperature may dip to below freezing in the winter.

August tends to be the warmest month of the year, while January and February are the coldest months. Most of the country experiences a rainy season from May to November. The northern coast, however, experiences this season from November to January. The heaviest rainfall generally occurs in May, while March is the driest month of the year.

The island of Hispaniola is centrally located in a tropical cyclone region, making the Dominican Republic particularly vulnerable to tropical storms. The country is struck about once every two years by a tropical storm or hurricane. The southern part of the country bears the brunt of these storms about 65 percent of the time.

SEARCHING FOR SUNKEN TREASURE

In Spanish colonial times, many Spanish ships sank during hurricanes near the present-day Dominican Republic. A few of these ships were loaded with treasures, and some people believe the treasures are still buried in the seafloor.
(A Closer Look, page 71)

Below: The Dominican Republic has beautiful beaches that are vulnerable to storms and hurricanes.

Plants and Animals

More than five thousand plant species grow in a variety of vegetation zones across the country. These vegetation zones include deserts, subtropical humid forests, and montane forests. The most common zone is the subtropical humid forest. This forest is easily identified by the presence of royal palm, mahogany, cashew, jagua palm, and satinwood trees. The country is also home to red and white mangrove forests.

The Dominican Republic has about three hundred bird species, twenty-seven of which are native to the country. Some notable birds are the Hispaniolan lizard-cuckoo, the burrowing owl, and the narrow-billed tody. The Hispaniolan solenodon and the Hispaniolan hutia are two of the most significant mammals that live on the island. Both animals are rarely seen because they are in danger of becoming extinct.

Above: **The Isla Cabritos National Park has one of the largest crocodile populations in the world.**

ENDANGERED SPECIES

The Dominican Republic has a number of endangered trees and animals. Conservation efforts are under way to prevent these species from becoming extinct.
(A Closer Look, page 60)

9

History

The Early Inhabitants — The Taino

The Taino, or Arawak, an indigenous people of the Caribbean region, lived in present-day Dominican Republic for as many as five thousand years before Christopher Columbus's arrival. The Taino practiced agriculture and fishing.

Christopher Columbus and Spanish Rule

Columbus's arrival in Hispaniola in 1492 marked the start of more than two hundred years of Spanish occupation and control. The first permanent Spanish settlement was at present-day Santo Domingo. The Spaniards worked to convert the Taino to Christianity and also enslaved many of them under the *encomienda* (ehn-koh-mee-EHN-dah) system, a Spanish legal system that gave Spaniards the right to force the locals to work for them. The Spaniards mined gold on Hispaniola, but by about 1520, they had exhausted the island's gold deposits. Most of the foreign settlers then left for Mexico, where large quantities of silver were discovered.

Left: Shown here is an artist's depiction of Taino people greeting Columbus when he landed on Hispaniola in 1492.

TOUSSAINT L'OUVERTURE

Toussaint L'Ouverture's original name was François Dominique Toussaint. The son of a learned slave, L'Ouverture learned how to read while serving as a household slave. In 1791, when a slave rebellion broke out, L'Ouverture founded a rebel group that used guerrilla warfare. In 1795, after France freed the slaves of Hispaniola, L'Ouverture fought on the side of France. In 1802, however, the French became wary that he had gained too much power, so they captured L'Ouverture and sent him to France. He was locked up there in an underground prison cell until his death on April 7, 1803.

SANTO DOMINGO

Santo Domingo is a historically significant city. During colonial times, the Spaniards used Santo Domingo as a base for their explorations into the rest of the Caribbean. In 1822, Haiti captured Santo Domingo to prevent outside forces from using the city as a base to attack Haiti.

(A Closer Look, page 66)

Between the French and the Haitians

In 1697, Spain ceded France the western third of Hispaniola, and the French named that section of the island Saint-Domingue. Over the next century, they developed Saint-Domingue into the richest sugar-producing colony in the world. The French imported slaves from Africa to work on their sugar plantations. These slaves were brutally treated, and in 1791, they coordinated a great slave rebellion. This rebellion led to a general revolt against French colonial power. In 1795, amid this revolt, Spain ceded France its portion of the island. French forces, under the leadership of Toussaint L'Ouverture, then worked to gain control of the entire island.

In 1804, however, the former Saint-Domingue declared its independence to become Haiti, and in 1809, the Spanish reclaimed their former territory to the east. In 1821, this territory enjoyed a brief independence from Spain until 1822, when Haiti invaded the eastern side of the island and added Santo Domingo to the Republic of Haiti. Haiti launched the invasion because it feared that the French wanted to reclaim Haiti through an attack on Santo Domingo.

The First Republic

Between 1822 and 1844, successive Haitian military governments controlled the whole of Hispaniola. People in the eastern part of the island were rendered powerless and began to resist Haitian rule. Juan Pablo Duarte, Francisco del Rosario Sanchez, and Ramon Matias Mella formed La Trinitaria, a political group, in response to the situation. La Trinitaria repeatedly attacked the Haitian army, and the Haitians eventually retreated. On February 27, 1844, the eastern side of the island officially declared its independence, and the first Dominican Republic was formed.

Above: The tomb of Duarte, Sanchez, and Mella is located on El Conde Street in Santo Domingo. The three men are called the "Founding Fathers of the Dominican Republic" for freeing the country from Haitian occupation.

The Spanish Return

Within six months, the leaders of La Trinitaria lost their power, and for the next seventy years, the country was ruled by *caudillos* (kaw-DEE-yohs), or military leaders. One such caudillo was General Pedro Santana. He asked the Spanish to retake control of their former colony in the hopes that Spain would provide the nation with financial support and military support against Haiti. Between 1861 and 1865, Spain briefly occupied the country, but in a series of struggles collectively known as the War of Restoration, the Dominicans resisted Spanish control. In 1865, Spain released the republic from its control.

Below: In 1844, Dominicans took part in a revolution that led to their independence from Haiti.

Left: **Woodrow Wilson (1856–1924) was the twenty-eighth president of the United States. He insisted that the Dominican Republic hold fair elections if the country did not want the presence of U.S. troops.**

United States Occupation (1916–1924)

More political, economic, and social chaos characterized the fifty-year period immediately following the War of Restoration. In 1905, concerned that the instability in the Dominican Republic posed a threat to U.S. trade and economic interests in the region, the U.S. government took over the management of the Dominican Republic's financial affairs.

Political unrest continued, however, and in 1914, President Woodrow Wilson threatened to send U.S. troops to the Dominican Republic if free and fair elections were not held. The Dominicans met this demand and elected Juan Isidro Jiménez as president. When a powerful Dominican general tried to remove Jiménez from office, the United States viewed the move as a coup, and the U.S. government sent in its military. In a short time, U.S. military personnel occupied every significant city in the country.

Between 1916 and 1924, the U.S. government, by way of the U.S. military, took over the Dominican government, banned the broadcast and publication of anything anti-American, and controlled the country's budget. During this period, however, political violence ended, and infrastructure and education improved. In 1924, the United States ended its occupation.

MILITARY PRESENCE

Dominicans resented the presence of the U.S. military in the Dominican Republic because military personnel abused their power at times. The military, however, improved living conditions in the Dominican Republic by building roads and schools and setting up Dominican infrastructure for communications. The U.S. occupation also contributed to economic growth in the Dominican Republic and partial settlement of the country's foreign debts.

The Road to Democracy

Between 1930 and 1961, ruthless dictator Rafael Leónidas Trujillo ruled the country until he was assassinated. Joaquín Balaguer, a puppet president under Trujillo, then took over as president for the next one and a half years. Juan Bosch succeeded Balaguer, but Bosch's liberal programs set the stage for a coup that soon ended his presidency.

On April 25, 1965, civil war broke out, and the U.S. government again intervened. U.S. troops entered the country to end the war, which the U.S. government believed was started by communists. In 1966 postwar elections, Balaguer was elected president. He managed to control further elections until 1978, when Antonio Guzmán of the Dominican Revolutionary Party was elected. Guzmán did not run for a second term and killed himself shortly before his term ended. Salvador Jorge Blanco then was elected and later was convicted of misusing funds.

In 1986, Balaguer returned as president and again manipulated elections to retain the presidency until 1994. After the 1994 elections, however, Balaguer shortened his stay in office in the face of domestic and international opposition against his misuse of the presidency. In 1996, the Dominican Republic experienced one of its fairest elections ever, and Dr. Leonel Fernandez Reyna of the Dominican Liberation Party won the presidency.

RAFAEL LEÓNIDAS TRUJILLO

For thirty-one years, Rafael Trujillo *(above)* ran an oppressive dictatorship in the Dominican Republic. In 1930, he became the country's president and brought unprecedented peace and prosperity to the country. Trujillo, however, also robbed the people of their civil liberties.

(A Closer Look, page 72)

Left: On March 3, 1967, Joaquín Balaguer, president of the Dominican Republic, delivered a speech.

Juan Pablo Duarte (1813–1876)

Juan Pablo Duarte is one of the "Founding Fathers of the Dominican Republic." In 1833, he returned from studying in Spain to find that Dominicans were unhappy with Haitian rule. Duarte established La Trinitaria with the aim of achieving independence and freedom from the Haitians. In 1844, he declared the country's independence but soon lost the new nation's presidency to General Pedro Santana, a military strongman. Duarte was forced to leave the country. He briefly returned during the War of Restoration.

Juan Pablo Duarte

Minerva Bernardino (1907–1998)

Minerva Bernardino was active in promoting women's rights for most of her life. She was involved in Accion Feminista Dominicana, a Dominican women's rights movement, and was one of the founding members of the United Nations Commission on the Status of Women. In 1946, she was one of only four women delegates to the first United Nations General Assembly. The four women wrote an "Open Letter to the Women of the World," which urged all women to be more active in politics and government.

Minerva Bernardino

Juan Bosch (1909–2001)

Juan Bosch is one of the Dominican Republic's most celebrated writers. He wrote about the hardships of the Dominican peasants during the Trujillo era. Bosch was forced to leave the country and lived in Cuba for twenty-four years because of his opposition to the Trujillo dictatorship. He wrote some of his most famous works while in exile, including *Dominican Dictatorships*, *Gold and Peace*, and *The Crafty One*. While in Cuba, Bosch helped form the Dominican Revolutionary Party and tried unsuccessfully to overthrow Trujillo. After Trujillo's assassination in 1961, Bosch returned to the Dominican Republic and worked to bring the political party to the country's peasants. In 1962, he won the presidency but lost it seven months later because his political ideologies were viewed as pro-communist. Bosch then was exiled again. He unsuccessfully ran for the presidency in the 1966 elections and in another five more elections up until 1994.

Juan Bosch

Government and the Economy

Representative Democracy

A president and a bicameral congress govern the Dominican Republic. The thirty-member Senate and the 149-member Chamber of Deputies form the National Congress.

The government consists of the executive, judicial, and legislative branches. The president and vice president exercise the power of the executive branch. Both the president and vice president are elected together by direct vote to serve four-year terms. President Hipólito Mejía and Vice President Milagros Ortiz Bosch won the 2000 elections. Bosch is the first woman to be elected vice president in Dominican history.

The Supreme Court of Justice heads the judicial branch, while Congress forms the legislative branch. The senators and deputies of Congress are elected by direct vote. The percentage of votes a political party receives determines how many seats that party will hold in Congress.

CONSTITUTION

The Trinitarians designed the first constitution of the Dominican Republic. On November 6, 1844, the constitution officially went into effect. Over the years, the country's constitution changed some thirty times. The numerous changes reflect the amount of political turmoil the country has experienced since its independence in 1844. Today, the country adheres to the revisions made to the constitution in 1966.

Local Government

The Dominican Republic is divided into twenty-nine provinces and one national district, which is located in Santo Domingo. Each province is controlled by a governor. All provincial governors are appointed by the president. The provinces are further divided into municipalities, each of which chooses its own mayor and council and is given some administrative freedom.

Military

The Dominican Republic has four branches of the military — the army, navy, air force, and national police. Dominican males must serve in the military sometime after reaching eighteen years of age. In 1998, the military expenditure was U.S. $180 million and made up 1.1 percent of the country's gross domestic product (GDP). From 1930 to 1961, Rafael Leónidas Trujillo used the military to ensure that he remained in power. In the 1990s, the military was put under civilian control in an effort to sanitize its bad reputation. The military's credibility, however, is still undermined by its members' involvement in drugs and corruption.

Above: Political banners and posters advertise candidates running in the next election.

POLITICAL PARTIES

Three major political parties compete for votes in the Dominican Republic. They are the Dominican Liberation Party, the Social Christian Reformist Party, and the Dominican Revolutionary Party.

Opposite: The Presidential Palace in Santo Domingo is famous for its lavish interior.

Shifting Economic Practices

Since the nation's independence, its economy has shifted emphasis from agriculture to services, which include tourism and finance. In 2001, the services sector accounted for 55 percent of the Dominican Republic's GDP. The Dominican Republic has an annual GDP of U.S. $50 billion. About 25 percent of the population, however, lives below the poverty level.

Free Trade Industrial Zones

In the 1980s, the manufacturing industry prospered with the increased number of free trade zones. Companies in these zones are not taxed by the Dominican government and so can operate at a low cost. The zones are located on the outskirts of Santo Domingo and other large cities. Factories in the free trade zones are often owned by foreign companies, such as Levi Strauss and Co., a U.S. business. The companies are attracted to the areas by the low operating costs. Facilities manufacturing items such as textiles and garments are concentrated in these zones. In 2001, goods produced in the free trade zones amounted to 85 percent of the Dominican Republic's total exports.

CASH CROPS

Although the agricultural industry has declined in importance, more fertile land is being allocated for the production of nontraditional crops, such as ornamental plants and fruits.

(*A Closer Look, page 52*)

Below: **Bananas are one of the most important cash crops in the Dominican Republic.**

Tourism

Tourism is a major industry in the Dominican Republic. The country's mountain and beach resorts and rich history and culture attract many tourists each year. In addition, the interior of the country offers ecotourism in the form of cave explorations, hikes, and excursions through the countryside and mountains.

In 2001, about 2.9 million tourists visited the Dominican Republic. Most of the tourists came from Europe and the United States. Since September 11, 2001, when the United States was struck by terrorist attacks, the Dominican Republic tourism industry has slowed in growth, but it shows signs of recovering. Between January and April 2003, the tourism sector contributed U.S. $900 million to the country's economy.

Overall, the Dominican economy is growing fast. Despite the drop in tourist earnings in 2001, the country's economic growth rate that year was still six times that of the rest of Latin America and the Caribbean.

Above: **The Dominican Republic's surrounding waters support various watersports activities. Tourism is centered in the coastal towns as well as in Santo Domingo, the capital city.**

People and Lifestyle

The Dominican Republic is a multiracial and multicultural nation, with a population of 8.7 million people. Over 60 percent of this population lives in and around the nation's cities. Dominicans are mainly of Spanish, African, or a mixture of Spanish and African descent. The country's culture and society, including its language and major religion, draw mainly upon its Spanish roots, although the music and dances of the country are heavily influenced by the people's African heritage.

Immigrant Population

The Dominican Republic is home to immigrants from many different countries. Most immigrants come from neighboring Haiti. Haitians come to the Dominican Republic to work in the sugarcane fields and make better lives for themselves. Unfortunately, Haitians are discriminated against, and the Dominican government has placed restrictions on Haitian immigration.

ANTIHAITIANISMO

Although the Dominican Republic and Haiti have shared the island of Hispaniola since the mid-1800s, relations between the two nations have always been uneasy. Haitians have long suffered antihaitianismo, or prejudice and discrimination against Haitians, in the Dominican Republic. Thousands of Haitians were brutally killed during the Trujillo years.
(A Closer Look, page 44)

Left: A Dominican soldier stands guard at the Haiti–Dominican Republic border, while a Haitian, carrying his belongings in a sack on his head, waits in the rain to enter the Dominican Republic.

The Social Classes

Dominican society is divided by a class structure. Less than 5 percent of Dominicans make up the "upper class," which includes Dominicans who have migrated to other countries, have become successful, and who occasionally return home. An example of these people are those who have become wealthy by playing for major league baseball teams in the United States.

About 35 percent of the population belongs to the "middle class." The middle class consists of professionals who work in the public or private sectors. Middle-class Dominicans do not have an independent means of income outside their employment, and their economic survival depends on the state of the economy and the availability of jobs.

The remaining 60 percent of the population makes up the "lower class." People from the lower class are poor because they do not have regular, well-paying employment. The lower class is further divided into urban and rural dwellers.

Above: **A man pounds rice outside his home in a rural part of the Dominican Republic. The rural poor often grow just enough food to feed their families.**

INCOME FOR THE URBAN POOR

The urban poor make their money in any way they can. Some become food vendors, shoe shiners, or cigarette and candy sellers. Others work as gardeners, maids, chauffeurs, or windshield cleaners at stoplights.

Family Life

Family ties are very important to Dominicans. The family unit acts as a foundation of support for its members when they need help, and relatives keep in close contact with each other. Two or three generations of Dominicans may live in the same household. In this situation, the oldest male often has the greatest authority. Dominicans also have relationships outside their family units based on *compadrazgo* (kohm-pah-DRAS-goh), a type of co-parentage or godparenting. In this type of relationship, the *compadre* (kohm-PAHD-reh), or godparent, plays an important role in the life of the godchild. Compadres are expected to help with the child's education, career, and finances.

Work Life

In 1998, the services sector and government employed an estimated 59 percent of the labor force, while industry and agriculture employed 24 percent and 17 percent of the labor force, respectively. As of 2001, about 15 percent of the population was unemployed.

Below: **A woman and her children spend an afternoon relaxing outside their home in Santiago. Rows of tobacco leaves hang outside the home to dry.**

Industrial free-trade zones are major areas of employment for Dominicans. Working conditions, however, are often poor in these zones, and workers are discouraged from joining labor unions.

Status of Women

In the Dominican culture, a woman often is expected to be as self-sacrificing and as dutiful as the Virgin Mary. This concept is called *marianismo* (mah-ree-ah-NEES-moh) and dates back to the Spanish colonial years. According to this ideal, women are expected to stay at home to look after their family members and cannot have an independent means of income. Although marianismo is still very much alive today, many poor women work because they have to in order to survive. Women are generally better educated than men because more women than men complete high school. Men may leave school before finishing their education to work and supplement the income for their families. Women, however, receive lower wages than men even when both are employed in similar occupations. Men are usually hired over women for the more skilled jobs.

Above: **Women in the Dominican Republic have a slightly longer life expectancy than men. Women on average live to be seventy-six years old, while men have an average lifespan of seventy-two years.**

Education

The Dominican Republic has both private and public schools. Many Dominicans are of the opinion that private schools offer the best education. Primary school education is free at public schools and is compulsory for children between the ages of seven and fourteen. After completing primary education, students go through a transitional two-year course followed by four years of secondary education. Secondary school is free, but students have to purchase their own textbooks. Upon completing secondary education, students can apply for university admission.

Only 70 percent of Dominican children attend primary schools. The remaining children do not have access to schools because they live in rural areas. In addition, some parents cannot afford to send their children to school because they need their children to work and help support the family.

Below: **Students have to undergo a two-year intermediate course before they can enroll in a secondary school.**

Higher Education

A combination of public and private universities offer higher education in the Dominican Republic. The only state-run university is the Universidad Autónoma de Santo Domingo, or Autonomous University of Santo Domingo. It is completely government-funded.

The government also provides partial funding to several private universities and institutions. The leading private universities include Universidad Nacíonal Pedro Henríquez Ureña, or Pedro Henríquez Ureña National University, and the Pontificia Universidad Católica Madre y Maestra, or Mother and Teacher Pontifical Catholic University. The Pedro Henríquez Ureña National University is a private university established in 1966 and located in Santo Domingo. The Mother and Teacher Pontifical Catholic University was set up in 1962.

Tuition fees are very low in the Dominican Republic. Many foreign students find the low fees attractive and travel to the country to complete their university education.

Above: **The Mother and Teacher Pontifical Catholic University has campuses in Santiago and Santo Domingo.**

AUTONOMOUS UNIVERSITY OF SANTO DOMINGO

The oldest university in the Dominican Republic is also the first university that was set up in the Western Hemisphere. This university was originally called Saint Thomas Aquinas.
(A Closer Look, page 46)

Religion

In 1954, Rafael Trujillo established Roman Catholicism as the official religion of the Dominican Republic. Trujillo sought to use the Church to preserve and add legitimacy to his dictatorship.

Roman Catholic practices in the Dominican Republic are often mixed with African folk beliefs. The Catholic Church, however, is the cornerstone of family life and is one of the ways families reconnect with each other. For example, events such as a child's baptism, a funeral, or a wedding will bring a family closer together. Officially, more than 90 percent of Dominicans are Catholics.

Other Christian denominations in the country include Seventh Day Adventist, Jehovah's Witness, Methodist, Baptist, and Mormon. A small Jewish population also exists.

Below: **The Church of St. Stanislaus is located in the village of Altos de Chavón. The village was built in the 1970s as a re-creation of a sixteenth-century European village. It has since become home to many Dominican artists and craftspeople.**

Traditional Beliefs

Many Catholics in the Dominican Republic combine their faith with traditional beliefs and practice Voodoo, Santeria, or Gagá. Voodoo and Santeria trace their origins to the Yoruba people of Africa. In the eighteenth and nineteenth centuries, Africans brought their own spiritual beliefs with them when they were sold as slaves in the West Indies. When colonists forced Yoruba slaves to convert to Roman Catholicism, the slaves did not completely abandon their folk beliefs to accept the new religion. Instead, they combined folk beliefs and Catholicism to form Santeria and Voodoo. In both Voodoo and Santeria, the identities of African deities and Catholic saints are merged. Voodoo has entered the Dominican Republic mainly through immigrants from Haiti, where this belief system is prevalent.

Gagá is a Dominican version of Voodoo. The religion is a mixture of Taino and African religious beliefs. Followers of Gagá play music and perform dances at their ceremonies. Gagá music is popular throughout the Caribbean and is commercially available on compact discs.

Above: **Many adult Haitians practice Voodoo. Voodoo is also known as Vodun, which comes from an African word that means "spirit."**

Language and Literature

Spanish, English, and Haitian Creole

Spanish is the official language of the Dominican Republic. English also is widely spoken because of the large number of Dominicans who emigrate to the United States and who regularly return to vacation in their homeland.

Haitian immigrants in the country communicate in Haitian Creole, a French-based Creole. This language is also spoken by some Dominicans, especially those who live in towns along the Haitian-Dominican Republic border.

HAITIAN CREOLE

Haitian Creole is a product of the French and African influences that molded Haiti's history. The language is a mix of French and African languages. Haitian Creole has six million speakers, the largest number of speakers among the Caribbean Creole languages.

Left: Spanish is the Dominican Republic's official language. The language is a legacy of the Spanish colonists, who came to Hispaniola in the fifteenth century.

Left: The Dominican Republic has a literacy rate of 82 percent. The rate is almost equal between men and women, with women having a slightly higher rate.

Literature and National Identity

The literary tradition of the Dominican Republic dates back to the beginning of Spanish occupation of Hispaniola. Dominican literature reflects the development of the country from Spanish and Haitian rule to independence. Today, much of the popular literature about the Dominican Republic comes from the immigrant Dominican community in the United States, and writers often focus on the hardships and frustrations of the people in their homeland.

Major Literary Movements

In the late nineteenth and early twentieth centuries, the country witnessed three literary movements. The first was *indigenismo* (in-dih-heh-NEES-moh), which worked to expose the brutalities the Taino experienced under the Spanish conquistadors. The second literary movement was *criollismo* (kree-oh-YEES-moh), which concerned itself with the Latin American lifestyles of the Dominican people. The third movement, appearing around 1921, was *postumismo* (pohs-tu-MEES-moh). This movement involves writing prose and poetry in a new style and breaks away from traditional literary styles.

DOMINICAN WRITERS

Manuel de Jesus Galván (1834–1910) and Juan Bosch (1909–2001) were among the respected Dominican writers of their times. Present-day writer Julia Alvarez is especially popular for *How the Garcia Girls Lost Their Accents*, a book she published in 1990.

Arts

Taino Art

Taino artifacts have been found in the Dominican Republic and other Caribbean countries during archaeological excavations and cave explorations. The artifacts include sculptures, ceramic pieces, pottery, and ornaments made from wood, shell, and bone.

Artistic expression was an important part of everyday Taino life. Everyday household items, for example, often were carefully made and highly decorated.

Painting

In the early twentieth century, Dominican artists broke away from traditional European subjects that had influenced their worked and began producing paintings with subjects that reflected

Left: **A Taino sculpture stands in a park in the Dominican Republic.**

Dominican heritage, lifestyle, and spiritual beliefs. Yoryi Morel and Celeste Woss y Gil were two of the prominent painters during this period.

Dominican art developed rapidly during Rafael Leónidas Trujillo's regime (1930–1961). Trujillo enjoyed paintings and encouraged artists in the Dominican Republic to pursue the art form. The growth of Dominican art during Trujillo's dictatorship was also boosted by the influence of Spanish artists who fled to the Dominican Republic during the Spanish Civil War (1936–1939). In 1942, Trujillo established the Escuela Nacional de Bellas Artes, or National School of Fine Arts, in Santo Domingo. The school has since produced many Dominican artists, including Fernando Ureña Rib and Julio Valdez.

In more recent years, Dominican art has become more experimental, and works often focus on the nation's social problems. Today, Rámon Oviedo is considered as one of the most important Dominican painters. Oviedo has won many awards and has participated in various exhibitions locally and abroad. He has painted several murals, including one in Washington, D.C.

Above: **The above painting was produced by François J. Amiel, a Haitian immigrant, in the year 2000.**

CULTURAL PLAZA

Paintings are among the artworks displayed in the Dominican Republic's Museum of Modern Art. The museum is located in Plaza de la Cultura, or Culture Plaza, which has a number of other museums and a theater that showcase different aspects of the nation's history and culture.
(*A Closer Look, page 56*)

Folk and Popular Music

The folk culture of the Dominican Republic has a rich tradition of ballads and chants. The country's folk music also reflects the nation's mixed heritage. Taino, African, and Spanish influences are evident in the type of instruments used, the type of songs sung, and the occasions on which songs are sung. Folk songs have various themes and purposes and include songs of social protest, songs for entertainment, children's songs, work songs, and religious songs.

Merengue became popular throughout the Dominican Republic in the twentieth century. Trujillo provided tremendous support for this lively music during his reign. Today, it is the most popular form of music in the country. One can hear merengue music played across the country in restaurants, public buses, and taxis. Other popular forms of music are salsa and *bachata* (bah-CHAH-tah), a type of slow, soulful music. Juan Luís Guerra is one internationally known Dominican musician who performs both bachata and merengue music.

Below: Traditional merengue bands feature an accordion, a two-sided drum, and a guiro *(left)*. Guiros were once made by the Taino out of hollow gourds, but they are now typically made out of brass cylinders. A guiro player scrapes the cylinder rhythmically with a special fork to make a buzzing or scratching sound.

Above: **Dominican women usually wear long skirts in folk dance performances.**

Folk Dances

Dominicans love to dance. The *sarandunga* (sah-rahn-DOONG-gah), bolero, *carabiné* (kah-rah-bee-NEH), and merengue (danced to merengue music) are all forms of Dominican dance. The sarandunga is a folk dance performed by many people at one time. The dance is accompanied by music performed on three small drums and a guiro, a percussion instrument formerly used by the Taino.

Both the carabiné and the bolero originated from Spanish dances. The bolero has since developed its own characteristics. This romantic and sentimental dance is performed slowly and smoothly. The carabiné has five variations and is accompanied by music played on an accordion, a guiro, and a tambourine. This complex dance involves changing partners, forming circles, and reversing the pattern of dance steps.

The merengue is the most popular dance form in the Dominican Republic. Once considered a dance for the rural and urban poor, it is now the national dance of the country.

MERENGUE

Merengue used to be associated with the poor. Trujillo changed this perception by introducing the dance to upper class members of Dominican society.
(A Closer Look, page 62)

Leisure and Festivals

Popular Pastime Activities

Dominicans enjoy swimming and relaxing on the country's many public beaches. Dominicans also are passionate about sports, including spectator sports such as cockfights and horseracing. Every major town and village in the country has a *gallera* (gah-YEH-rah), or cockfighting pit, and cockfights are popular among urban and rural people alike. In Santo Domingo, cockfights are also attended by the upper class.

Horses

In urban areas, horseracing is a well-attended spectator sport. Horseraces are held several times a week at the Perla Antillana and V Centenario hippodromes in Santo Domingo. Many Dominicans also go horseback riding in their spare time, and most farmers survey their properties on horseback.

COCKFIGHTS

Cockfights are popular and usually held on weekends. People often bet money during cockfights.
(A Closer Look, page 54)

Below: Horseback riding is an activity Dominicans enjoy everywhere — through mountains, along beaches, and in jungles.

Socializing and Dominoes

To relax, Dominicans often meet family or friends at public parks or plazas. Such visits are a common form of socializing in the Dominican Republic. In rural areas, women and children normally return directly home from work or school to prepare dinner for the men of the household. Men, on the other hand, frequently visit with friends after work to play games such as cards, pool, and dominoes.

Dominoes involves four players and uses small rectangular blocks divided into two sections. Each section may be blank or marked with between one to six dots. Play begins when the first player lays down a block. The next player then must lay down a match against either end of that block. A match is a block with a section that matches, in number of dots, a section of the previous players' blocks. Play continues until one player has laid down his or her last block, winning the game.

Above: **In the Dominican Republic, domino tables can be seen on patios, in bars, and at street corners. Men may play a game of dominoes for hours, especially on weekends.**

35

Baseball

Béisbol (BAYS-bohl), or baseball, is an important sport in the Dominican Republic. The country has six professional baseball teams and various baseball stadiums and fields. The government pays for the building of stadiums and neighborhood fields, as well as for coaches' salaries, to maintain the country's production of good baseball players. The professional baseball season in the Dominican Republic lasts from October to February. Major games are usually held in Santo Domingo, and they are attended by thousands of baseball enthusiasts.

Basketball

Most Dominican youths enjoy basketball and play the sport throughout the year. Although basketball is not as popular as baseball, a steady following for basketball exists throughout the Dominican Republic. The professional basketball season lasts from June to August. Tournaments are held for different age groups starting from as young as ten years of age.

BASEBALL

Baseball is seen as a way to break out of poverty in the Dominican Republic. A number of Dominican baseball players have become wealthy playing in the U.S. major leagues. One of them, Alex Rodriguez, signed the largest contract in sports history in 2000.
(A Closer Look, page 48)

Below: Baseball is the national passion, and children often play the game in their neighborhoods.

Nature Walks

Some Dominicans enjoy going for hikes and walks in the country. The Dominican Republic has mountains, valleys, forests, and beaches that encourage such outdoor activities. Adventurous Dominicans climb Pico Duarte every year on February 27 to celebrate Independence Day. The mountain is the highest in the country. Pico Duarte is named after Juan Pablo Duarte, who helped liberate the Dominican Republic from Haiti.

Sportfishing

Dominicans enjoy fishing in Samaná Bay, Mona Passage, and the waters near Saona Island and La Romana. A large variety of saltwater fish can be caught at these locations. The fish include marlin, barracuda, dorado, sailfish, tuna, kingfish, red snapper, wahoos, and groupers. Some marlin weigh as much as 1,000 pounds (454 kilograms), while wahoos can weigh up to 150 pounds (68 kg). Summer is the best time for sportfishing in the Dominican Republic.

Above: **Fish such as the barracuda (*above*), the wahoo, and the dorado can be caught in Dominican waters throughout the year.**

Carnivals

Carnival in the Dominican Republic dates back to colonial times when the residents of Santo Domingo would put on costumes and walk the streets of the town. The event once occurred on the eve of Lent. Today, Dominicans celebrate Carnival in both February and August to mark independence from Haiti and Spain, respectively. The February Carnival is the larger of the two celebrations. Various towns also have specific dates on which they celebrate their own Carnival.

Carnival is an exciting and noisy event in the Dominican Republic. Most people participate in the event with the aim of having the best possible time. Creative costumes and elaborate masks are the trademarks of the Dominican Carnival, and the event is the most colorful celebration in the country.

Carnival celebrations are filled with music and parades of dancers, bands, and floats decorated with flowers and banners. Crowds of people flood the streets and dance to the lively music of merengue bands.

CARNIVAL

The entire Dominican Republic celebrates during Carnival time. Dominicans take great care and pride in designing their masks and costumes, which are prominent features of the celebration.
(*A Closer Look*, page 50)

Below: **Beauty queens walk through the streets of La Vega during the Carnival parade in February.**

Christmas

The Christmas season lasts from December 15 to January 6. Many parties and family gatherings are held during this season. On Christmas Eve, people eat a traditional Christmas dinner at home. This dinner usually consists of a meat and vegetable stew or roasted pork. Dominicans then attend midnight mass in their respective community churches.

Children open presents on the final day of the Christmas season. Dominicans remember January 6 as the day that the Three Kings went to look for baby Jesus. On the night of January 5, children place boxes of grass under their beds to wait for the arrival of the Three Kings on their camels. The children hope that the camels will eat the grass from under their beds and the Kings will leave Christmas presents for them.

Food

Food in the Dominican Republic is often fresh. People grow or catch most of the food that they eat. Dominican fare is a mix of Taino, Spanish, and African cooking methods and ingredients. As a result, Dominican food is full of color, flavor, and spice.

Main Dishes

The Dominican Republic's national dish is called *sancocho* (sahn-KOH-choh), a Dominican version of the Spanish *cocido* (koh-THEE-doh), or stew. Often served on special occasions, the dish is typically a combination of various meats and vegetables made into a stew. Another local favorite is *la bandera* (lah bahn-DEH-rah), or "the flag," which consists of white rice, red beans, and fried green plantains. La bandera is served with stewed meats such as chicken, beef, or mutton. Breakfast varies across the country. In the poor regions, breakfast often consists of *mangu* (mahn-GOO), a puree made from cassava, a starchy root. In cities, breakfast may consist of bread, jam, and coffee. Lunch is the largest meal of the day. Rice and beans with meat is the favorite for this meal. Supper is served after all members of the family have returned home from work or school.

Left: Dominicans enjoy roasted pork and often roast a pig for Christmas Eve dinner.

Left: The Dominican Republic has a rich marine life. Seafood, such as lobster, is commonly available and sold fresh in the country's restaurants and markets.

Snacks and Desserts

Dominicans enjoy snacks. Many Dominican snacks are made locally and often cannot be found outside of the Dominican Republic. The most common snack is the *pastelito* (pahs-teh-LEE-toh), a turnover filled with meat. Served at celebrations and sold on streets, the pastelito is a traditional snack enjoyed by all Dominicans. Other traditional snacks are *quipes* (KEE-pehs), or fried cracked wheat and ground beef; *fritos de batata* (FREE-tohs deh bah-TAH-tah), or fried sweet potatoes; *fritos maduros* (FREE-tohs mah-DOO-rohs), or fried ripe plantains; *platanitos* (plah-tah-NEE-tohs), or green plantain chips; and *yaniqueques* (jah-nih-KEH-kehs), or cornmeal cakes.

Dominican desserts are very sweet. These desserts are locally made and, like Dominican snacks, often cannot be found outside of the country. Popular desserts include *arroz con leche* (ahr-ROHS kohn LEH-cheh), or milk and rice pudding; and *dulce de leche cortada* (DOOL-cheh deh LEH-cheh kohr-TAH-dah), or sour milk cream. Dulce de leche cortada is similar to yogurt.

SWEET TREATS

The Dominican Republic has other delicious and unusual desserts, such as sesame seed and molasses candy, ginger and cassava bread pudding, and guava shells in syrup.

A CLOSER LOOK AT THE DOMINICAN REPUBLIC

The Dominican Republic has a rich culture that has been influenced by its history of Spanish colonialism and Haitian and U.S. occupation. The Dominican Republic's national language is Spanish, and the country's national sport is baseball. In fact, some 23 percent of U.S. major league baseball players are from Latin America, and the majority of those are from the Dominican Republic. Apart from its baseball stars, the Dominican Republic is also known for its capital city, Santo Domingo, the oldest and second-largest city in the Caribbean.

Opposite: **The Presidential Palace is located on Calle de las Damas, the main street in Santo Domingo. This street is lined with several buildings of historical significance.**

The country is famous for merengue, a distinctive Dominican music and dance. The Dominican Republic has also attracted treasure seekers to its surrounding seas, where sixteenth-century Spanish ships wrecked and scattered their treasures.

The country has had dark periods in its history. Between 1930 and 1961, dictator Rafael Trujillo ruled the Dominican Republic with an iron fist. He kept most of the nation's wealth for himself and ordered the killings of Haitian immigrants in the country.

Above: **Beach vendors sell all kinds of goods to tourists, from brightly colored paintings and sculptures to freshly cooked lobsters.**

Antihaitianismo

Antihaitianismo, or prejudice against Haitians, in Dominican society grew over a series of historical events. One of the earliest instances dates back to the 1700s, when Saint-Domingue (present-day Haiti), a French colony, imported thousands of African slaves. The use of slaves increased agricultural production, and the colony soon became wealthy. The Spanish elite in the present-day Dominican Republic feared their own loss of power to the wealthy French and began a campaign that preached separation from everything French, however faintly related.

In 1804, Haiti became independent and the world's first free black republic. To protect their own interests, Santo Domingo's Spanish elite then encouraged racial discrimination disguised as nationalism. They spread ideas of nationhood that defined the rightful people of the Dominican Republic as white, Roman Catholic, and of Spanish descent. The Haitians became regarded as the most undesirable because they posed the sharpest contrast to these characteristics. They were portrayed as a dark-skinned people who practiced traditional African religions and who had adopted certain French influences.

THE HAITIAN OCCUPATION

Between 1822 and 1844, Haitian forces occupied Santo Domingo. Bitter at their loss of power and prestige, many elite Dominican families left Hispaniola to settle elsewhere. Those who stayed often harbored hatred from having to answer to Haitian people, whom they considered inferior. In 1844, the Dominican elite regained power when the Dominican Republic formally became independent. Although initial attempts by Haitian forces to reclaim their former territories served to fuel antihaitianismo, racist sentiments were perpetuated, particularly in literature and government policies, long after the Haitians retreated. These racist sentiments were used by ruling Dominicans to unite the country's people as a group, distinct from Haitians.

Left: In the 1700s, African slaves were brought to Saint-Domingue to work on sugarcane plantations.

Left: **A Haitian child carries a container on her head as she walks through a sugarcane plantation.**

Antihaitianismo Today

Anti-Haitian sentiments are evident in everyday Dominican life. Although antihaitianismo is no longer part of official government policies, elements of anti-Haitian racism continue to be taught in schools and perpetuated through the country's mass media.

Haitians living in the country have few rights. According to the Dominican Republic's constitution, children born in Dominican territory to Haitian parents are entitled to citizenship. Children of Haitian immigrants, however, are often not given birth certificates by authorities who discriminate against Haitians. These children are then at risk of being deported to Haiti on the grounds of being illegal immigrants. Dominico-Haitians typically also face difficulties in obtaining education and health care. In 2001, about one million Haitians were estimated to be living and working in the Dominican Republic.

CHILD IMMIGRANTS

Besides by legal immigration, Haitian children also enter the Dominican Republic illegally through human smuggling operations. These children work as street vendors or laborers upon reaching the country. Some of them become beggars.

Autonomous University of Santo Domingo

The Autonomous University of Santo Domingo began in the early sixteenth century as an educational center founded by Roman Catholic missionaries of the Order of Saint Dominic. Fray Pedro de Córdoba headed the order. The order eventually asked the Pope to grant the rank of university to the center because of the studies it provided. On October 28, 1538, the Pope agreed to their request, creating the first university in the Western Hemisphere. The university was named Saint Thomas Aquinas. The university has since been renamed the Universidad Autónoma de Santo Domingo, or Autonomous University of Santo Domingo.

The university's administration was once autonomous, or independent of the government. Today, the Autonomous University of Santo Domingo is the country's only public university, and it is funded entirely by the government. Over the years, the university's student population has fluctuated. In 1984, an estimated 100,000 students were enrolled at the university. In 1990, the number of students dropped to about 40,000. In 1995, the number rose to 65,000 students. In 2000, the number of students stood at 125,000.

Below: **University students take a break on campus grounds in between lectures.**

International Programs

The Autonomous University of Santo Domingo is involved in several international agreements to expand higher education in the Dominican Republic. The university's student exchange program with Oita Medical University in Japan and the university's participation in an agreement between the Dominican government and the Ohio Agricultural Research and Development Center (OARDC) are two such agreements.

In 1989, the government of the Dominican Republic signed an agreement with Japan's Oita Medical University to allow the Autonomous University to participate and assist in research projects supported by the Japanese university.

In 2003, the OARDC and the Dominican government signed a $1.25-million contract that promised student and faculty exchanges between the center and three Dominican universities. The Autonomous University of Santo Domingo is one of the three universities. The project helps to build master's degree programs in soil science and other sciences in Dominican universities. According to the contract, fourteen Dominican students will be trained and will graduate with a master of science degree.

Above: **A young Dominican tends to crops on a farm. Agriculture is an important part of the Dominican Republic's economy, and the country has signed an agreement with a U.S. agricultural research organization to improve agricultural education in the Dominican Republic.**

Baseball

Baseball was first introduced to the Dominican Republic by Cuban immigrants fleeing Cuba during the Ten Years' War (1868–1878) and seeking refuge in the country. The immigrants had learned the game from U.S. sailors stationed in Cuba and brought the sport with them to their new country. Dominicans soon learned the game and formed their own baseball teams. Four professional baseball teams were founded during the first half of the twentieth century, and these teams have become the oldest teams in Dominican baseball.

Baseball Dreams

Today, baseball is the Dominican Republic's national sport. A baseball diamond can be found in almost every town in the country. Young Dominican boys can attend baseball training camps if they are interested in becoming professional baseball players. Good players are then selected to play for the national teams. Competition is high for the few places on the teams.

THE FIRST FOUR BASEBALL TEAMS

Between 1907 and 1936, the Dominican Republic saw the birth of its first four baseball teams. In 1907, Tigers del Licey (The Tigers) was formed in Santo Domingo. In 1911, Estrelles Orientals (Eastern Stars) from San Pedro was born. In 1921, Santo Domingo created its second team, Leon del Escogido (Lions of the Chosen One). Santiago also formed a baseball team that same year and named it Sandino. In 1936, Sandino was renamed Las Anguilas (The Eagles). All four baseball teams are still playing today.

Left: Thousands of fans watch a baseball game as fireworks go off over the stadium.

Left: On April 26, 2003, Chicago Cubs player Sammy Sosa waved to the crowd during a game against the Colorado Rockies in Denver, Colorado.

Many Dominican boys hope to become professional players one day. Some see baseball as a way to escape poverty. Baseball heroes inspire such a hope. One such Dominican hero is Samuel Peralta Sosa, better known as Sammy Sosa. Sosa was born into a poor family. To play baseball, young Sosa made his own bat and glove out of a tree branch and milk cartons, respectively. When he was sixteen, Sosa was scouted by the Texas Rangers to play professional baseball. He was traded to the Chicago White Sox and then to the Chicago Cubs.

Sosa is one of many Dominican baseball players who are successful in professional baseball. Today, 23 percent of all U.S. major league baseball players are from Latin America. Most of these players come from the coastal towns in the southeastern region of the Dominican Republic. The Dominican Republic also now has six national teams playing in the country's own professional baseball league.

DOMINICAN STARS

Apart from Sammy Sosa, players such as Pedro Martinez (Boston Red Sox) and Alex Rodriguez (Texas Rangers) are a source of Dominican national pride. In 2000, Rodriguez signed a ten-year contract worth $252 million with the Texas Rangers. The contract is the largest in sports history. The first Dominican to play major league baseball in the United States was Ozzie Virgil, who began playing for the New York Giants in 1956.

49

Carnival

Carnival is a traditional celebration in the Dominican Republic. This outdoor event takes place twice a year, first in February and the beginning of March and also in mid-August. The largest Carnival celebrations in the country take place in the cities of Santo Domingo, Santiago, and La Vega.

The most important part of Carnival celebrations is the costumes. People spend a lot of time designing and dressing up in creative costumes. The costumes are made of brightly colored fabrics and decorated with small, shiny objects, such as bells and mirrors. Costumes often have matching masks. Many masks represent folk characters.

Carnival Masks

Carnival celebrations throughout the Dominican Republic feature an interesting array of folk characters. Some are frightening, while others are funny. The main character of Carnival is the

Right: **Death and devil costumes are common in Carnival festivities. The main purpose of these costumes is to frighten bystanders.**

Below: **A woman in a colorful costume and headdress dances in a Carnival celebration.**

devil, known by different names in different parts of the country. People who go to Carnival celebrations dressed as the devil wear ugly masks with two long horns and sharp teeth or a snout.

A National Celebration

Originally, Carnival was a European religious celebration before the Christian season called Lent. Lent is a time of fasting and penance in preparation for Holy Week, which ends with Good Friday and Easter. Carnival was a chance for people to enjoy a lot of food and fun before Lent began. When the Spaniards colonized the present-day Dominican Republic in the late fifteenth century, they brought their Carnival traditions with them.

For Dominicans, Carnival later became not only a religious event but also a national celebration. On February 27, 1844, the Dominican Republic gained independence from Haiti, and on August 16, it regained its independence from Spain. These two events have now become major reasons for Carnival celebrations.

MASK DECOR

Carnival masks are a traditional art form in the Dominican Republic. They are handmade, and some have unique features. A devil mask, for example, may have horns decorated with flowers *(below)*.

Cash Crops

Agriculture generally employs some 17 percent of the Dominican population. During the 1970s and the 1980s, this sector of the economy declined in importance as the service sector began to play a more important role. In the late 1980s, the government tried to diversify the nation's crops and set aside land for growing nontraditional crops, such as ornamental plants and citrus fruits. The programs, however, have been slow in taking effect, and today, the traditional cash crops are still the main focus of the agricultural sector.

Sugarcane

In the sixteenth century, the Spaniards introduced sugarcane to the region. It was only in the nineteenth century, however, that sugar production began to flourish in the country, following investments from U.S. sugar companies. In 1959, the Dominican Republic became the main supplier of sugar to the United States. In the 1980s, however, this heavy reliance on sugar hurt the nation's economy when world sugar prices dropped. The situation worsened when sugar orders from the United States fell and artificial sweeteners began to be developed. Sugar, however, is still the nation's main agricultural export.

TOBACCO

In the 1960s, the introduction of new varieties of tobacco and an increase in international tobacco prices helped the Dominican Republic's tobacco industry. Tobacco sales in the country peaked in 1978 but then dropped in the 1980s due to diseased crops and a drop in prices. The country also has one of the highest numbers of smokers in Latin America, and smoking-related diseases such as cancer have been on the rise.

Below: **Haitian immigrants make up the majority of the labor force in Dominican sugarcane fields.**

Coffee and Cacao

In 1715, coffee was introduced to the region, and it is now the Dominican Republic's second-most important crop. Similar to sugar, coffee production has experienced various problems. Instead of large, more efficient plantations, the coffee industry has been based on small farms that produce small amounts of coffee. In addition, international coffee prices have changed rapidly. In the 1980s, the International Coffee Organization placed tighter restrictions, or quotas, on how much coffee the country could sell abroad, and its revenue from coffee fell. To make up for lost income, coffee farmers are beginning to specialize in more expensive gourmet and organic coffees.

Cocoa beans come from the cacao tree. Cocoa was first produced in the Dominican Republic in the 1880s. In the 1970s, the production of cocoa expanded rapidly due to high world prices. In 1987, the country earned $66 million in cacao-related exports and became the Caribbean's largest producer of cocoa. The industry, however, often suffers from inefficient production and problems with quality control. In 2002, Dominican cacao exports amounted to only $9.9 million.

Above: **Coffee beans grow in clusters and usually turn red when they are ripe.**

Cockfights

Cockfighting is a traditional pastime in the Dominican Republic and is enjoyed by Dominicans in both urban and rural areas. Cockfights are held in arenas or cockfighting pits called galleras. The most famous gallera is Santo Domingo's Alberto Bonetti Burgos Cockfighting Coliseum, which caters to members of the middle and upper classes. Cockfights are usually held on Sundays. On Sundays, the galleras in the country are often crowded with eager spectators, most of whom are men. Many spectators place bets on which cock will win a fight.

The Fighters

The cock is believed to be a descendent of the Indian red jungle fowl. Gamecocks are specially bred and trained so that they can participate in a fight. On the day of a fight, a *gallero* (gah-YEH-roh), or handler, will have his gamecock weighed and color tagged. Cocks of the same age and weight are usually pitted against each other. The cock is identified by the color of his tag during a fight, and spectators place bets on their favorite "color."

Below: **A Dominican man shows off his gamecock while waiting for its turn to fight in the gallera.**

Origin of Cockfights

Cockfights have been popular in east Asian countries since ancient times. In Bali, Indonesia, cockfighting is more than just a sport or gambling opportunity. It is part of an important religious ritual in some Hindu temples.

Above: **A man shows excitement when his gamecocks jump at each other at the Alberto Bonetti Burgos Cockfighting Coliseum in Santo Domingo.**

Cockfighting was introduced to Greece around 524 B.C. and later spread to Rome and the rest of Europe, including Spain and its colonies, such as Hispaniola. By the sixteenth century, English royalty had grown fond of the sport, and the British later brought cockfighting to their colonies in North America.

Cockfights are also popular in Haiti and, like in the Dominican Republic, they are usually held on Sundays there. In addition to winning money, a Haitian gamecock handler may enjoy a higher status in Haitian society if his gamecocks win their fights.

Animal Cruelty

Although cockfighting is a popular sport in the Dominican Republic, the issue of cruelty toward animals is an ever-present one. Cockfighting is legal in the Dominican Republic, but in places such as Canada, Britain, and most of the United States, the sport is banned due to laws against animal cruelty.

Cultural Plaza

The Plaza de la Cultura, or Cultural Plaza, is located near the center of Santo Domingo. As its name suggests, the site is a cultural center, and it includes four museums and the national theater. The museums are the Museo del Hombre Dominicano (Museum of the Dominican Man), Museo de Arte Moderno (Museum of Modern Art), Museo Nacional de Historia Natural (National Museum of Natural History), and Museo Nacional de Historia y Geografía (National Museum of History and Geography).

Museums

Considered to be the most interesting museum in the Dominican Republic, the Museum of the Dominican Man showcases the history of the Dominican people from before Columbus's arrival to modern times. The Museum of Modern Art maintains a

Below: **The Museum of the Dominican Man was founded in 1973. The museum displays artifacts left behind by the Taino, by Spanish settlers, and by African slaves.**

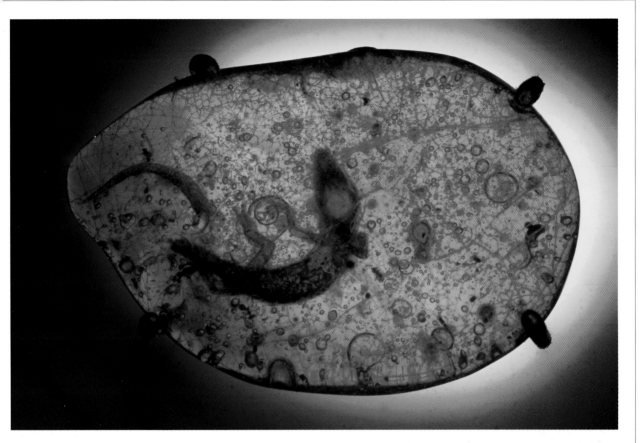

permanent collection of Dominican art and organizes temporary exhibits of work by local, Caribbean, and international artists. Exhibits in the National Museum of Natural History focus on the formation and mining of amber, the geographical history of plants and animals in the country, the nation's different forest zones, and the various animal species found in these zones.

The National Museum of History and Geography focuses on the Dominican Republic's history. A section of the museum concentrates on dictator Rafael Trujillo, and the car that he was killed in is one of the exhibits in this section.

Above: **Dominican amber is regarded as some of the finest amber in the world. The lizard in this piece of amber serves to increase the stone's value.**

National Theater

The National Theater was opened in 1973 and consists of two auditoriums with a combined seating of about 1,800 people. The larger of the two auditoriums is called Sala Principal and can hold up to 1,600 people. Each year, Santo Domingo's finest dance, music, and drama performances are held in Sala Principal. The smaller auditorium, Sala Revelo, can hold 175 people and is mainly used for speaking events and conferences.

BEAUTY PAGEANTS

The National Theater is used to stage the Miss Dominican Republic pageant, from which the nation's Miss World and Miss Universe representatives are selected. Eighteen-year-old Amelia Vega won the 2003 Miss Universe title for the Dominican Republic. This contest was held in Panama.

Dominican Cigars

The Taino, who smoked rolled tobacco leaves during religious ceremonies, were among the first to cultivate tobacco. The practice of smoking later spread to the Spanish explorers who arrived on Hispaniola. In the 1600s, the explorers introduced tobacco to Spain and Portugal when they returned to their homelands. From there, tobacco smoking spread to France and England.

The History of Cigars

In 1717, the first cigar manufacturing factory opened in Seville, Spain. Tobacco was imported from the Spanish colony of Cuba and rolled into cigars in the Seville factories. The colony of Cuba began producing its own cigars in 1821.

Cigars became popular in the United States around the 1860s, and the U.S. demand for Cuban cigars was high. Almost a century later in 1959, the Cuban government implemented policies with which the United States disagreed. In 1962, the United States banned the import of all Cuban goods, including Cuba's famous

Below: Dried tobacco leaves are sorted according to age. Old leaves have a stronger flavor, while young leaves are more elastic and easier to roll.

Above: **Neatly arranged cigars dominate the shelves of this shop in Playa Dorado Shopping Plaza, near Puerto Plata.**

cigars. As a result, several cigar companies operating in Cuba took their businesses and expertise to the Dominican Republic, where the industry flourished. Today, the Dominican Republic is the world's largest producer of handmade cigars. Prestigious brands, such as Davidoff, Avo, Arturo Fuente, and Romeo y Julieta, contain tobacco grown in the Dominican Republic.

The Dominican Cigar Industry

Tobacco is grown in the northern regions of the country near the city of Santiago. In 1990, about 3 percent of arable land was used for growing tobacco. The country's Instituto del Tabaco de la Republica Dominicana, which was started in 1962, studies how to increase tobacco production and keeps track of tobacco quality.

The largest market for Dominican cigars is the United States. About half of the handmade cigars sold in the United States come from the Dominican Republic. Americans who smoke cigars generally prefer light tobacco blends.

HEALTH STUDY

In 2002, the University of Rochester Medical Center in the United States began a five-year research project on smoking in the Dominican Republic. The project aims to educate Dominicans on the health dangers of smoking and to cut down the number of smokers in the country.

Endangered Species

Almost all of the Dominican Republic's large animals and many of its smaller ones are endangered. The Dominican government has outlawed many practices that endanger animals or their habitats, but enforcing the laws has been difficult. National parks have been created to protect the natural habitats of many species, but some species continue to decrease in number since the government is often unable to prevent poaching or human encroachment into animal habitats. According to the World Conservation Union (IUCN), the luth, Hispaniolan hawk, bay-breasted cuckoo, black-capped petrel, Hispaniolan solenodon, Ricord's iguana, and La Selle thrush are some of the endangered and critically endangered animals in the Dominican Republic.

ENDANGERED TREE SPECIES

Animal species are not the only species that face the danger of extinction. Some plant species in the Dominican Republic are also endangered. The guaiac and the West Indian mahogany are two of the trees that have been listed as endangered or critically endangered in the Dominican Republic.

Left: Poaching, or the illegal hunting of animals, is a serious problem in the Dominican Republic. Sea turtles, which are endangered animals, are often killed for their meat.

Conservation Projects

The Dominican government is cooperating with international organizations on several conservation projects to protect the future of some of the nation's endangered and critically endangered species. The projects include efforts to save the Ricord's iguana from possible extinction.

Ricord's Iguana

The Iguana Specialist Group of the IUCN has been working with groups in the United States and the Caribbean to protect the habitat of the Caribbean iguanas. In the Dominican Republic, Ricord's iguana is known to live only in the Neiba Valley and on the Barahona Peninsula. The iguana population is on the decline. Experts estimate only two thousand to four thousand iguanas exist in the wild. The clearing of vegetation for agricultural use or fuel and the overgrazing of the area by cattle are threatening the iguanas' existence. The Ricord's iguana receives partial protection in the Neiba Valley region, while iguanas in the Barahona Peninsula range are protected in a national park and reserve.

Above: Animals which are not native to the island, such as cats, dogs, and mongooses, further endanger Hispaniola's iguanas by feeding on them. Dominicans also have a taste for iguana, and they serve iguana meat in a few specialty dishes.

Merengue

The merengue dance is often considered the Dominican Republic's national dance. The dance uses fast steps, and it is usually performed by a man and a woman in close contact.

The Birth of Merengue

The merengue is believed to have first emerged in the Dominican Republic in the nineteenth century. One of the most famous composers of merengue music is Juan Bautista Alfonseca (1810–1875). His greatgrandson, Luis Felipe Alberti (1906–1976), also became a great composer.

Initially, only people in rural areas enjoyed merengue. People from the upper classes considered both merengue music and dance uncultured. During his dictatorship between 1930 and 1961, however, Rafael Trujillo changed upper-class sentiments toward merengue. Trujillo promoted merengue music and dance in order to win the favor of rural people. He brought merengue

Below: **Merengue music is played by a band that uses instruments such as the accordion; the *tambora* (tahm-BOH-rah), a drum that can be hit on either side with the hand or a stick; and the guiro, a rough metal cylinder that a musician plays by scraping it with a stick.**

bands to ballrooms where upper-class Dominicans held grand social events. During this period, merengue bands added the sounds of the piano and trumpet to their music, creating a type of "big band" merengue music. Big band merengue was slower than traditional merengue. After Trujillo's assassination in 1961, however, merengue bands once again became smaller.

Above: **Merengue is the country's most popular dance and is enjoyed by people of all ages and social classes.**

Modern Merengue

Today, people of any social class in the Dominican Republic dance to merengue music anywhere — in ballrooms, in dance clubs, and in street festivals. In the Dominican Republic, large orchestras as well as small bands are dedicated to merengue music. Dominicans listen to merengue music on the radio, watch merengue dance on television, and enjoy the merengue live at music festivals and Carnival celebrations. The merengue is also popular outside of the Dominican Republic. Modern variations of the merengue have fused the music with other musical styles, such as salsa and jazz, to produce new rhythms.

MERENGUE FESTIVALS

The Dominican Republic holds merengue festivals every year. During these festivals, people dance to music played by the country's best merengue musicians and bands. The largest merengue festival takes place in Santo Domingo during the end of July and the beginning of August.

National Parks

The Dominican Republic has more than sixty parks and reserves that are protected by law. These areas have a variety of climates and habitats and protect many plant and animal species, some of which are endangered. The National Parks Office, located in Santo Domingo, is in charge of overseeing these protected areas.

Jaragua

The largest national park in the Dominican Republic is Jaragua National Park, in the southwestern part of the country. The Jaragua landscape includes forests, islands, and lagoons. Most of the plant life in the park consists of cacti, which do not need much rain. The park's lagoons support mangrove trees.

The largest flamingo community in the country lives in the lagoons of Jaragua, especially in the Oviedo lagoon. The park is also home to herons, great egrets, ibis, spoonbills, and terns, among other birds. Bats, iguanas, sea turtles, and snakes are some of the other animals living in Jaragua.

Left: Some national parks in the Dominican Republic contain mangroves. This mangrove forest at Samaná Bay is one of the largest mangrove forests in the Caribbean Basin.

Left: Flamingos can be found in the Jaragua and Isla Cabritos national parks and on Saona Island, which is located near the southeastern part of the country.

Isla Cabritos

The Isla Cabritos National Park is an island in Lake Enriquillo in southwestern Dominican Republic. The park is home to many birds and reptiles, including the burrowing owl and the endangered Ricord's iguana. Isla Cabritos also has one of the largest crocodile populations in the world.

Armando Bermúdez and José del Carmen Ramírez

The Armando Bermúdez and José del Carmen Ramírez national parks border each other and together cover 612 square miles (1,585 square km) of mountainous terrain. The tallest mountains in the country, including the 10,417-foot (3,175-m) Pico Duarte, are found in these two parks. Some of the Dominican Republic's major rivers, such as Yaque del Norte, begin in these mountains.

Different species of plants and trees grow at different levels on the slopes of the parks' mountains. Pine trees predominate on the higher slopes, while cedar, juniper, and olive trees are more common lower down.

Birds such as crows, doves, parrots, and woodpeckers make their homes in the trees of the Armando Bermúdez and José del Carmen Ramírez national parks. Iguanas, wild pigs, and snakes are other animals that can be found in the parks.

ECOTOURISM

Tourists visit the national parks of the Dominican Republic to bird-watch or enjoy outdoor activities such as mountain hiking and whitewater rafting. More importantly, the parks are the last refuges for plants and animals that have shrinking natural habitats. The National Parks Office promotes ecotourism as a way to let people enjoy the natural beauty of the Dominican Republic without causing too much environmental damage.

Santo Domingo

The First City in the New World

In 1496, Bartholomew Columbus, brother of explorer Christopher Columbus, founded Nueva Isabela, the first permanent European settlement in the Western Hemisphere. Located on the eastern bank of the Ozama River, Nueva Isabela was soon destroyed by a hurricane. In 1502, the city was rebuilt on the other side of the river and renamed Santo Domingo. With a base in the "New World," the Spanish began exploring and colonizing nearby islands and parts of North and South America.

A History of Foreign Domination

In 1586, Sir Francis Drake, an English explorer and soldier, led attacks on Santo Domingo and other Spanish settlements in the region. Drake had the blessings of the English Crown. Later, in 1655, British troops tried to capture Santo Domingo but were defeated by the city's people, who united to resist them.

From 1795 to 1809, however, the French took control of the city during an uprising against Spanish rule. Later, the Haitians ruled the city from 1822 to 1844. In 1844, when the country gained independence from Haiti, Santo Domingo was declared the

CIUDAD TRUJILLO

In 1930, Santo Domingo was destroyed by a hurricane. The city was rebuilt, and between 1936 and 1961, Santo Domingo was known as Ciudad Trujillo, or Trujillo City. Rafael Trujillo changed the name of the city to honor himself. The city's original name was restored after the dictator's death.

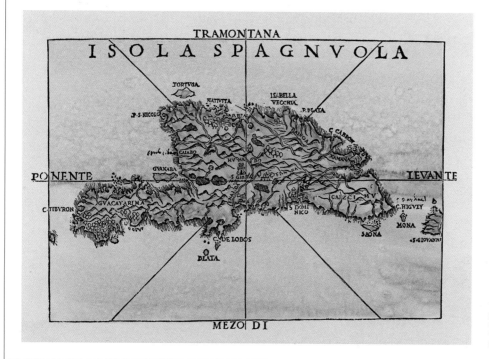

Left: Peter Martyr D'Anghiera and Gonzalo Fernandez de Oviedo y Valdez drew this 1534 map of Hispaniola. Both men were Spanish historians in the sixteenth century.

capital city of the newly formed Dominican Republic. For a brief period after independence (1861–1865), the Dominican Republic again came under Spanish rule. Since 1865, however, Santo Domingo has been the Dominican Republic's capital city.

Above: **In 2003, the bustling city of Santo Domingo hosted the Pan American Games, in which several thousand athletes from various countries participated.**

Santo Domingo Today

Santo Domingo in the twenty-first century has a population of more than 2.5 million people, and it is a lively mix of old architecture and modern structures. The city's colonial past is vividly apparent due to the many sixteenth-century structures, such as the palace of Diego Columbus, the Ozama Fort, and the Tower of Homage, that are still standing. In 1990, the colonial portion of Santo Domingo was declared a World Heritage Site by UNESCO. The city welcomes tourists to its historical sites and offers visitors world-class hotels and shopping centers.

The more modern side of Santo Domingo includes the Dominican Republic's main financial institutions and industries. The city's many factories produce petrochemicals, metal products, and consumer goods, including processed food, refrigerators, and textiles. The city is also home to the country's main seaport, which is located at the mouth of the Ozama River.

Sea Creatures

Migratory Whales

The ocean waters surrounding the Dominican Republic are home to some of the world's most interesting sea creatures. From December to April each year, several thousand humpback whales migrate from the chilly North Atlantic waters to the Caribbean. In these warmer waters, the whales mate and bear young. The main breeding and birthing grounds in Dominican waters are along Silver Bank and Christmas Bank and in Samaná Bay.

In October 1986, President Joaquín Balaguer declared Silver Bank a protected humpback whale sanctuary. The sanctuary was enlarged in 1996 to include Christmas Bank and Samaná Bay.

Whale-Watching

Regular whale-watching tours in the Dominican Republic began in the late 1980s. Today, the tours are usually conducted from January to March and cater mostly to foreigners. Since January 1992, the Dominican government has imposed a tax on every

Below: **The city of Samaná has a museum that displays marine artifacts such as this whale skeleton.**

person who goes on a whale-watching tour. This tax helps pay for monitoring and controlling the number of whale watchers in the area and also brings in extra revenue for the government.

Above: **Instead of a shell, the leatherback turtle has thick, leathery skin on its back.**

Other Sea Creatures

Manatees are found in Samaná Bay and in Neiba Bay, near Barahona. These mammals are popularly known as "sea cows" because they chew on water plants for hours, and they can weigh up to 1,300 pounds (600 kg). Manatees rarely stray from their homes and live peacefully in small family groups.

Leatherback, green, loggerhead, and hawksbill sea turtles also live in the waters around the Dominican Republic. All four species are endangered. The leatherback sea turtle is the largest of the sea turtles and can weigh up to 1,200 pounds (540 kg). The green sea turtle is named for its color and is the fastest swimmer among the sea-turtle species in its region. The hawksbill sea turtle has a hooked upper jaw that resembles a hawk's beak. The loggerhead sea turtle gets its name from its large head and short, wide neck. It also has a set of powerful jaws that help it trap and eat smaller hard-shelled animals, such as clams and crabs.

Searching for Sunken Treasure

Spanish Shipwrecks

From the sixteenth to the eighteenth centuries, the Spanish colonized areas of the Americas and the Caribbean. Ships left Spain with trade supplies for the colonies and returned loaded with goods.

Many ships never made it back to Spain because they were either attacked by pirates or destroyed in hurricanes. Only a few of the hundreds of Spanish ships that sank during this period were loaded with "treasure." The riches on these ships included gold and silver mined in Colombia, Peru, and Mexico, as well as jewels from other colonies. One such ship, *Nuestra Señora de la Concepción*, set sail from Cuba for Spain loaded with coins and other valuable cargo. The *Nuestra Señora de la Concepción* ran into a hurricane off the Florida coast, turned back, and lost its crew and cargo at a reef near the Dominican Republic. The area where the ship wrecked was named Silver Bank for the treasures that were lost there.

Salvage Operations

In the colonial period, Spanish authorities organized salvage operations to recover lost cargo. Upon receiving news of a shipwreck, salvage fleets traveled to the site of the wreck and often used Native divers to recover lost cargo.

One of the earliest tools used in these salvage efforts was the diving bell, which enabled divers to spend more time underwater. The bell was lowered vertically from a ship and submerged in the water to capture air in its upper part. Divers entered the bell to breathe, rest, and observe their surroundings before continuing their work.

In recent decades, advances in diving and underwater recovery equipment have led to an increase in Caribbean salvaging efforts. Popular among salvagers are the waters surrounding the Dominican Republic, where they have found colonial coins. In most cases, salvagers keep a small portion of their findings, while the Dominican government retains the larger portion. Items most commonly found are Spanish colonial coins.

COLONIAL MINT

Coins from the Spanish-American colonial period were irregular in appearance and shape due to they way they were made. To make a coin, a chunk of silver was cut from a silver bar or slab and given a value according to its weight (the lower the weight, the higher the value). This piece was then heated and placed between two molds. With a pound of a hammer, the molds' patterns were imprinted onto either side of the piece. The molds, however, did not give a definite shape to the resulting coin, and not all of their patterns were imprinted. Each coin, then, was unique, with its value based on weight rather than appearance.

Opposite: **Many ships have been wrecked in Hispaniolan waters, including Christopher Columbus's ship, *Santa Maria*. On December 24, 1492, Columbus left an inexperienced crew in charge of the ship as he slept. Strong currents stranded the ship on a reef early the next morning.**

Rafael Leónidas Trujillo

Born in 1891 to José Trujillo Valdez, a postmaster, and Altagracia Julia Molina, a homemaker, Rafael Leónidas Trujillo Molina was the third of eleven children (five boys and six girls). His family was relatively poor and lived in San Cristóbal, where he was born.

A Career Soldier Turns Corrupt

The U.S. occupation of the Dominican Republic began when Trujillo was twenty-five years old, and he joined the U.S. Marine Corps training program two years later, in 1918. Trujillo rose swiftly through the ranks, and, by 1927, he had become a general. In 1930, Trujillo was part of a military coup that overthrew the Dominican president at that time, Horacio Vásquez. For the next thirty-one years, Trujillo ruled the Dominican Republic with an iron fist while engaging in a series of self-serving schemes. Trujillo used the country's resources to build a personal financial empire. Every part of this empire was operated and supervised by a member of his immediate or extended family. Trujillo was also

TRUJILLO EMPIRE

Apart from benefiting himself and his family, Trujillo's economic policies mainly benefited the Dominican Republic's wealthy elite.

His projects included developing the country's industries and building its infrastructure. Initially, these projects seemed to be geared toward improving the lives of the country's people. As time wore on, however, it became clear that this was not the case. Wealth generated from the Dominican Republic's economy was not evenly distributed and was enriching mostly Trujillo's family. By the late 1950s, it is widely believed that much of the Dominican economy was directly controlled by either Trujillo or a member of his family.

Left: **At a banquet on August 23, 1958, General Rafael Leónidas Trujillo** (*right*) **speaks to his son Rafael Trujillo Jr.**

ruthless toward any political opposition he faced. During his rule, dissidents were exiled, imprisoned, tortured, or assassinated. Near the end of Trujillo's rule, the country's prisons became overcrowded with political prisoners. In May 1961, Trujillo was assassinated by members of the Dominican military.

Above: **Trujillo was driving this car to his San Cristóbal farm when he was shot and killed by assassins.**

Dominicanization

In the 1930s, Trujillo introduced a racist immigration scheme that favored people with fairer skin and persecuted Haitians, who were generally perceived as having darker skin. The scheme has since been known as "Dominicanization."

In 1937, after Haiti's ailing economy had driven many of its citizens across the border into the Dominican Republic to work as laborers on sugarcane fields, Trujillo ordered the slaughter of every Haitian in the land. Tens of thousands died in a few days. Trujillo then undertook propaganda efforts to portray his scheme as one that was defending the country and its people from undesirable foreign influences. Trujillo engaged the help of Dominican writers Manual Arturo Peña Batlle and Joaquín Balaguer for his campaign. Trujillo's desire to decrease the proportion of the population that was of African descent also led him to welcome European immigrants.

JEWISH IMMIGRANTS

In the late 1930s, Trujillo received Jewish European immigrants with open arms. Historians speculate that this move served his racist purposes and also placed him in a favorable light on the international stage because many larger and wealthier countries turned away Jewish immigrants.

RELATIONS WITH NORTH AMERICA

The Dominican Republic has always maintained close relations with North America. In the nineteenth century, the United States developed economic ties with the Dominican Republic by investing in the Dominican sugar industry. Between 1916 and 1924 and again in 1965, the United States occupied the country and intervened in the local political environment. The United States's moves caused a strain in its relationship with the Dominican Republic. Although sometimes resentful of the United States's intervention in their nation's affairs, Dominicans

Opposite: **At a cockfighting pit in Santo Domingo, two men use recycled Coca-Cola bottles to sell drinks. Trade between the Dominican Republic and the United States is extensive.**

Above: **Tourists from North America and Europe make up the largest number of tourists entering the Dominican Republic.**

depend greatly on the United States politically and economically. A large Dominican immigrant community in North America also draws the Dominican Republic and the continent closer together. The Dominican immigrant community in North America maintains close ties to its homeland through family and business connections, as well as through an active Dominican research community in the United States. In the last few years, the United States and the Dominican Republic have become more mutually supportive of each other's causes.

Economic and Political Bases

The United States's interest in the Dominican Republic began when U.S. companies started investing in the Dominican sugar industry in the nineteenth century. The U.S. government later became concerned about the Dominican Republic when its unstable political climate was viewed as a threat to U.S. businesses in the country and to U.S. national security. The United States also wanted to limit European influences in this nearby country. In 1916, the United States used these perceived threats as a basis for intervening in and occupying the Dominican Republic.

Although the U.S. occupation ended in 1924, the U.S. government still had political interest in the nation because of the Dominican Republic's geographical closeness. In 1965, the Dominican Republic underwent another period of political chaos. The United States again entered the country briefly because it believed that communists were causing the political uprisings. Through a succession of presidents, the United States has remained a concerned neighbor of the Dominican Republic.

POLITICAL INFLUENCE

The United States has historically wielded influence over Dominican politics. In 1962, Juan Bosch was elected president but was soon ousted by the Dominican Republic's military. The U.S. government, which was wary of Bosch's communist policies, did not help the elected president recover power, and, later, in 1965, the U.S. government intervened when Bosch supporters were fighting a civil war to restore him to power. In the Dominican Republic's 1978 elections, on the other hand, pressure from the U.S. government enabled Antonio Guzmán to be elected, despite the Dominican military's opposition to Guzmán and its attempts to halt the election.

Left: U.S. military personnel drive down a street in Santo Domingo during the U.S. occupation of the Dominican Republic in 1965.

Left: **On May 20, 2003, Dominican president Hipólito Mejía and U.S. president George W. Bush met at the White House to discuss relations between the two countries.**

Trade Relations with the United States

The United States has been an important trade partner for the Dominican Republic. In 1970, the United States received 83 percent of Dominican exports. That percentage, however, fell to 52 percent in 1980 and then increased to 87 percent in 1987. These fluctuating percentages reflect the country's past, unstable dependence on a single export — sugar. The country is now attempting to move away from this dependence and diversify its exports, but it is also becoming more and more dependent on the U.S. market for its exports. In 2002, the United States received 87 percent of the Dominican Republic's exports.

Much of the country's imports come from the United States. In 2000, 60 percent of its imports were from the United States. Three-quarters of its agricultural imports are also from the United States. In 2001, the Dominican Republic received U.S. agricultural imports worth U.S. $603 million. These imported goods included snack foods, processed fruits, cotton, and tobacco.

The Dominican Republic has made several trade agreements with the United States. These agreements include the U.S. Generalized System of Preferences and the Caribbean Basin Initiative (CBI).

HUMAN INTEREST

The United States and the Dominican Republic are working together to combat drug abuse and human smuggling activities in the Dominican Republic. In 2002, the U.S. government contributed U.S. $1.3 million to the Dominican Republic's antidrug campaign. The U.S. Department of State also granted U.S. $80,000 to the International Organization for Migration to aid its efforts against the trafficking of humans into the Dominican Republic.

Caribbean Basin Initiative

In 1983, the U.S. Congress passed the Caribbean Recovery Act, their first of three acts that eventually would make up the Caribbean Basin Initiative (CBI). The CBI is a major U.S. foreign economic project that mainly involves Central American and Caribbean countries. Under the initiative, a variety of goods from the twenty-four participating countries can be sold in the U.S. market duty-free, or without taxes. The CBI also encourages U.S. businesses to invest in Caribbean countries.

The Dominican Republic has benefited from this program, especially from the duty-free entry of some of its clothing and textiles into the United States. Textiles are now one of the country's main exports. Also, U.S. investment in the Dominican Republic has increased. U.S. companies are particularly attracted to the country's free trade zones.

CHIEF BENEFICIARY

The Dominican Republic is the chief consumer of benefits available under the CBI. Other participants in the CBI include Haiti, Jamaica, Panama, Honduras, the Bahamas, Barbados, El Salvador, Aruba, and Costa Rica.

Left: **On May 18, 2000, U.S. president Bill Clinton** *(center)* **signed the Trade and Development Act into law on the South Lawn of the White House as members of Congress stood by. The law includes the Africa Growth and Opportunity Act and the United States-Caribbean Basin Trade Partnership Act, which is now part of the CBI.**

The Peace Corps

Volunteers of the United States Peace Corps have been coming to the Dominican Republic since 1962. The country has received help from these volunteers in key areas such as health, education, the environment, and urban and rural development.

In 1965, Peace Corps volunteers stayed in the Dominican Republic when civil war erupted in the country. The volunteers remained in troubled areas to treat the war's wounded. In 1979, volunteers also provided disaster relief when the country was hit by hurricanes David and Frederick. Local Dominicans as well as the Dominican government have shown the volunteers honor, affection, and gratitude. In 1986, the Peace Corps received the Dominican Republic's highest medal for its work.

The Peace Corp celebrated its fortieth anniversary in 2002. In the Dominican Republic, this celebration was attended by President Hipólito Méjia, Vice President Milagros Ortiz Bosch, and baseball celebrity Sammy Sosa. In 2002, there were about 150 Peace Corps volunteers in the Dominican Republic.

Below: **During the civil war in 1965, Peace Corps nurse Arleen Serino** (*far left*) **from the Bronx, New York, attended to a woman who lost her leg in a mortar shell explosion. The explosion happened at a hospital near the Duarte Bridge in Santo Domingo.**

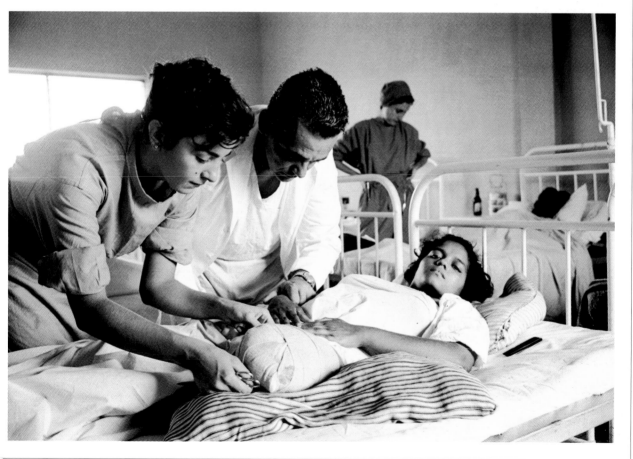

USAID

The United States Agency for International Development (USAID) is the section of the U.S. government responsible for providing monetary help to other countries for various national projects in those countries.

The Dominican Republic benefits from USAID in the areas of education, health, the economy, the environment, and disaster relief. USAID also pairs up nongovernmental organizations (NGOs) with an international organization that works to prevent corruption.

USAID now is working to ensure that Dominicans get a regular supply of electricity. The Dominican Republic has a limited capacity for electricity generation and, as a result, it suffers frequent power outages. In 1989, the government-run Corporación Dominicana de Electricidad (CDE) provided electricity generation and distribution in the Dominican Republic. This company, however, could not meet the country's rising demand for electricity. In 1999, the Dominican Republic privatized, or sold to privately owned companies, its electricity sector. USAID believes that this move will help improve the power infrastructure in the Dominican Republic. USAID is helping the country regulate the newly privatized industry.

RURAL ELECTRICITY

An estimated four hundred thousand houses in the rural areas of the Dominican Republic do not receive electricity. Benedicto, located in the eastern part of the country, was one village in these rural areas. In 2001, Benedicto received electricity for the first time as a result of joint efforts by USAID, the National Rural Electric Cooperative Association (NRECA), and AES, a private electricity distributor.

MONETARY AID

Every year, the Dominican Republic receives about $235 million from USAID.

Left: On June 19, 2002, security guards stood outside the door of AES, a major Dominican electricity supplier, in anticipation of a demonstration by locals. Power outages happen often enough to frustrate residents and stall productive economic activities.

Left: On April 21, 2001, Canadian prime minister Jean Chretien received Dominican Republic president Hipólito Mejía in Quebec City, Canada, after the third Summit of the Americas.

Free Trade Agreement

In March 2002, Canada and the Dominican Republic began to explore the idea of a free trade agreement between the two countries. Canada views the agreement as a positive step ahead in the country's economic and political relationship with the Dominican Republic. The agreement would also be helpful in opening the rest of the Caribbean region to Canadian investment. Combined trade between the Dominican Republic and Canada was estimated at CAN $245 million in 2002, and the Dominican Republic estimates that Canadian investment in the country is close to U.S. $1.4 billion.

Canadian-Dominican Commerce

The Canadian-Dominican Chamber of Commerce has been involved in the Dominican Republic and Canada since 1987. The chamber has more than one hundred members and has offices located in Santo Domingo. The group was founded by several Dominicans and Canadians who wished to promote Canadian-Dominican relations. The organization encourages two-way trade, economic projects, and cultural exchanges between Canada and the Dominican Republic.

CANADIAN EXPORTS

The Dominican Republic is Canada's largest market for its imports in the Caribbean. In 2002, Canada exported goods to the Dominican Republic that were worth CAN $127 million. The goods consisted mainly of food, paper products, and electrical and automobile items.

Immigration to North America

Dominicans have been immigrating to North America since the early nineteenth century. After 1965, immigration to the United States increased when the United States relaxed its laws to allow entry to immigrants coming to join their family members already settled in the country.

Essentially, Dominicans immigrate to the United States to find better jobs to support themselves and their families. To Dominicans, prospects seem brighter in the United States, and they usually are able to get jobs that pay better than what they have been earning in the Dominican Republic. Generally, only about one-third of Dominican immigrants do not have a job in their native country before emigrating.

Besides the search for jobs, Dominicans also emigrate to further their studies or to unite with family members who are already settled in North America. Ten percent of the entire Dominican-born population now lives in the United States. Most of these immigrants live in New York City and other coastal cities of the southern and eastern United States.

Below: **On April 17, 1996, Salustiano Gutierrez** *(front row, second from right)* **of the Dominican Republic joins more than 1,500 other immigrants to the United States in reciting the Oath of Allegiance.**

Dominicans in the United States

More than one million Dominican immigrants live and work in the United States. In the 1980s and 1990s, they were the fastest-growing ethnic group in New York City and formed the second-largest Hispanic group.

Many Dominicans in the United States, including those in New York, gain blue-collar employment in sectors such as manufacturing. In the 1970s and 1980s, however, the manufacturing sector in New York City shrunk and left many Dominicans unemployed. In 1989, the employed Dominicans earned an income that was half the average income rate in New York City. A 1997 study found that Dominican immigrants were among the poorest groups of people in the city, with almost half of the population living below the poverty line. Despite this situation, Dominicans are diligent about sending money back to their families in their native country. Among developing countries, the Dominican Republic is one of the top ten recipients of remittances from the United States. In 2001, the remittances amounted close to U.S. $2 million and formed 9 percent of the Dominican Republic's Gross Domestic Product (GDP).

A 1994 amendment to the Dominican constitution allows Dominicans who have emigrated to keep their Dominican nationality. A dual nationality allows these Dominicans to vote during elections held in the Dominican Republic.

MIGRATION CALL

The Dominican Republic has seen increased trade, economic growth, and humanitarian and financial help from foreign countries. Despite improved economic conditions in the Dominican Republic, Dominicans still aspire to emigrate to other countries such as the United States. Many Dominicans see the United States as a place to earn a living and the Dominican Republic as the place in which they will retire.

Dominican Interest Groups

Some Dominicans are concerned about the growing number of poor Dominicans living in the United States, and they worry about the future of the Dominican immigrant community. A number of Dominican interest and lobby groups have been formed to look out for the interest of Dominican Americans.

One such group is the Dominican-American National Roundtable (DANR), an independent and nonprofit group that attempts to bring together the immigrant Dominican population in the United States. The group aims to make sure that all Dominican Americans are aware of their rights as citizens of the United States. In late 2002, the DANR proposed a Dominican-American Caucus in the United States House of Representatives. The group believes that such a caucus will provide better representation for the Dominican immigrant population in the U.S. government.

Other Dominican interest groups in the United States include Alianza Dominicana. This group provides a number of services, including child and family welfare services, to the Dominican immigrant community in New York City. Quisqueya in Action is a nonprofit group that strives to increase a national understanding of Dominican cultural and traditional values. The group was formed in 1987 and has since established various programs for

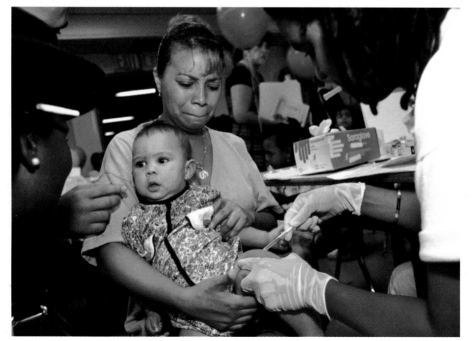

RESEARCH GROUP

The Dominican Studies Institute at the City University of New York (CUNY) produces, collects, and distributes information about Dominicans worldwide. Apart from conducting research, the group sponsors conferences and forms an effective bridge in bringing together experts from universities and members of the immigrant community.

Left: At a health fair in the Washington Heights neighborhood in New York City, a woman winces as a medical worker immunizes her baby. Washington Heights contains the largest community of Dominicans in the United States.

Dominican-American parents and their children. The Group of Dominican Professionals in Washington, D.C., is a nonprofit group formed to unite professional Dominicans living in the Washington metropolitan area.

Dominican-New York Grief

On November 12, 2001, an airplane bound for the Dominican Republic crashed just three minutes after its takeoff from the John F. Kennedy International Airport in New York City. The crash of American Airlines Flight 587 was due to mechanical problems. All 260 people on board the plane died. Most of the passengers were Dominicans who worked in New York and were going back to their country to visit family members. At least two of the crash victims escaped the terrorist attacks on the World Trade Center just two months before. The Dominican community lost forty-one lives in the September 11, 2001, attacks.

Grieving relatives and friends of the victims filled the airport in Santo Domingo in the Dominican Republic as soon as they heard of the accident. The U.S. Embassy in the Dominican Republic helped these Dominicans travel to the United States to identify and claim the bodies. The situation was more complicated for Dominicans who were living illegally in New York City, because coming forward to claim the bodies of their loved ones would expose their unauthorized status in the country.

ROCKAWAY

American Airlines Flight 587 nosedived into Rockaway, in the borough of Queens, New York City. The area is just 15 miles (24 km) from the site of the September 11, 2001, terrorist attacks. Rockaway was also the home of many firefighters and police officers who died in the World Trade Center rescue operations.

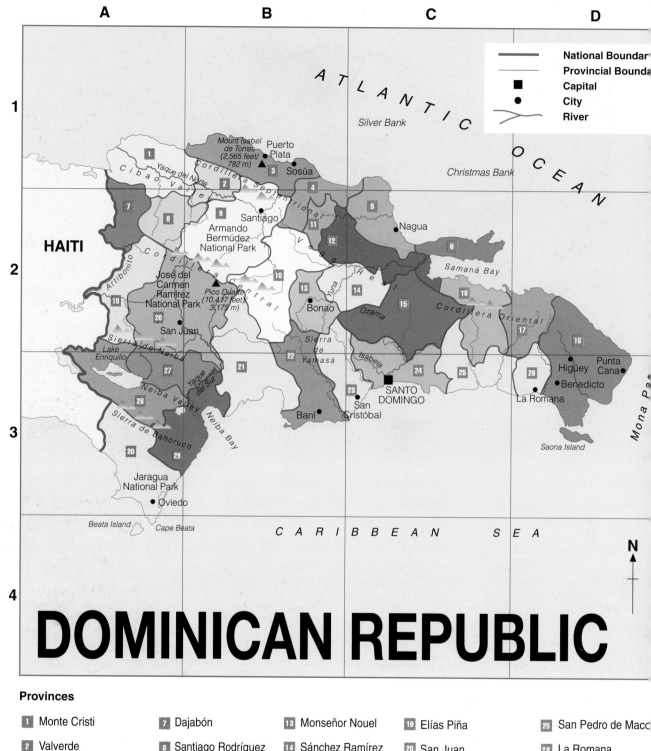

DOMINICAN REPUBLIC

A B C D

1

2

3

4

ATLANTIC OCEAN

Silver Bank

Christmas Bank

National Boundar
Provincial Bounda
Capital
City
River

Mount Isabel de Torres (2,565 feet/ 782 m)
Puerto Plata
Sosúa

HAITI

Cibao Valley
Yaque del Norte
Cordillera Septentrional
Santiago
Armando Bermúdez National Park
Vega Real
Nagua
Samaná Bay

Artibonito
Cordillera Central
José del Carmen Ramírez National Park
Pico Duarte (10,417 feet/ 3,175 m)
Bonao
Yuna
Ozama
Cordillera Oriental

San Juan
Sierra del Neiba
Lake Enriquillo
Sierra de Yamasá
Isabela
SANTO DOMINGO
Higüey
Punta Cana
Benedicto
La Romana

Neiba Valley
Yaque del Sur
Neiba Bay
Baní
San Cristóbal
Mona Pas

Sierra de Bahoruco
Jaragua National Park
Oviedo
Saona Island

Beata Island
Cape Beata

CARIBBEAN SEA

N

Provinces

1 Monte Cristi
2 Valverde
3 Puerto Plata
4 Espaillat
5 María Trinidad Sánchez
6 Samaná

7 Dajabón
8 Santiago Rodríguez
9 Santiago
10 La Vega
11 Salcedo
12 Duarte

13 Monseñor Nouel
14 Sánchez Ramírez
15 Monte Plata
16 Hato Mayor
17 El Seibo
18 La Altagracia

19 Elías Piña
20 San Juan
21 Azua
22 Peravia
23 San Cristóbal
24 Distrito Nacional

25 San Pedro de Maco
26 La Romana
27 Bahoruco
28 Independencia
29 Barahona
30 Pedernales

Above: Petrochemical plants are located near the Ozama River in Santo Domingo.

Armando Bermúdez
  National Park B2
Artibonito River A2
Atlantic Ocean A1–D2

Baní B3
Beata Island A4
Benedicto D3
Bonao B2

Cape Beata A4
Caribbean Sea A3–D4
Christmas Bank C1–D2
Cibao Valley A1–B2
Cordillera Central
  A2–B2
Cordillera Oriental
  C2–D2
Cordillera
  Septentrional
  B1–B2

Haiti A1–A3
Higüey D3

Isabela River C2–C3

Jaragua National
  Park A3
José del Carmen
  Ramírez National
  Park A2–B2

La Romana D3
Lake Enriquillo A3

Mona Passage D2–D3
Mount Isabel de
  Torres B1

Nagua C2
Neiba Bay B3
Neiba Valley A3–B3

Oviedo A3
Ozama River C2–C3

Pico Duarte B2
Puerto Plata B1

Punta Cana D3

Samaná Bay C2
San Cristóbal C3
San Juan A2
Santiago B2
Santo Domingo C3
Saona Island D3
Sierra de Bahoruco
  A3–B3
Sierra de Neiba A2–A3

Sierra de Yamasá B2–B3
Silver Bank C1
Sosúa B1

Vega Real B2–C2

Yaque del Norte River
  A1–B2
Yaque del Sur River
  A3–B3
Yuna River B2–C2

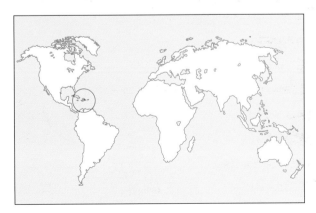

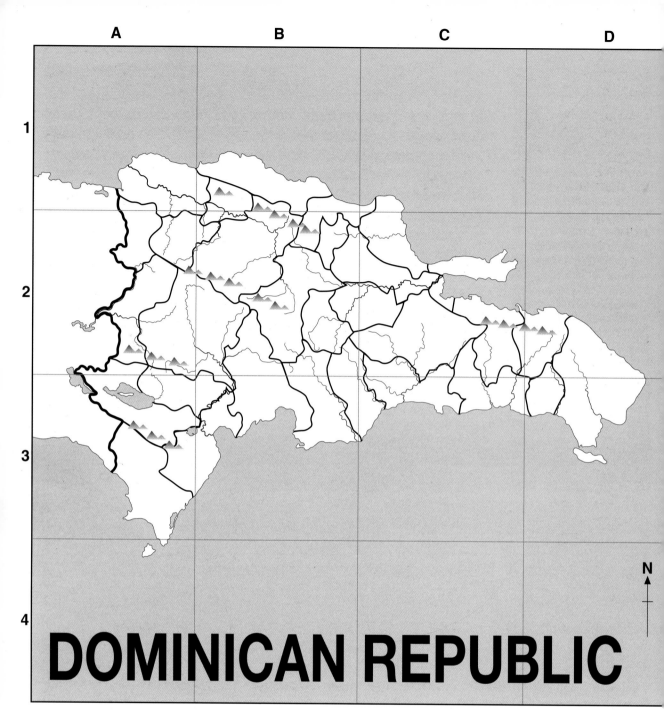

A **B** **C** **D**

1

2

3

4

DOMINICAN REPUBLIC

N

Above: **The Dominican Republic has many beautiful beaches.**

How Is Your Geography?

Learning to identify the main geographical areas and points of a country can be challenging. Although it may seem difficult at first to memorize the locations and spellings of major cities or the names of mountain ranges, rivers, deserts, lakes, and other prominent physical features, the end result of this effort can be very rewarding. Places you previously did not know existed will suddenly come to life when referred to in world news, whether in newspapers, television reports, other books and reference sources, or on the Internet. This knowledge will make you feel a bit closer to the rest of the world, with its fascinating variety of cultures and physical geography.

This map can be duplicated for use in a classroom. (PLEASE DO NOT WRITE IN THIS BOOK!) Students can then fill in any requested information on their individual map copies. The student can also make a copy of the map and use it as a study tool to practice identifying place names and geographical features on his or her own.

Dominican Republic at a Glance

Official Name   Dominican Republic

Capital   Santo Domingo

Official Language   Spanish

Population   8.7 million

Land Area   18,810 square miles (48,730 square km)

Provinces   Azua, Bahoruco, Barahona, Dajabón, Distrito Nacional, Duarte, Elías Piña, El Seibo, Espaillat, Hato Mayor, Independencia, La Altagracia, La Romana, La Vega, María Trinidad Sánchez, Monseñor Nouel, Monte Cristi, Monte Plata, Pedernales, Peravia, Puerto Plata, Salcedo, Samaná, Sánchez Ramírez, San Cristóbal, San Juan, San Pedro de Macorís, Santiago, Santiago Rodríguez, Valverde.

Major Leaders   Juan Pablo Duarte (1813-1876)

Rafael Trujillo (1891-1961)

Joaquín Balaguer (1906-2002)

Juan Bosch (1909-2001)

Highest Point   Pico Duarte 10,417 feet (3,175 m)

Major Rivers   Yaque del Norte, Yaque del Sur, Ozama

Major Lake   Lake Enriquillo

Major Highlands   Cordillera Septentrional, Cordillera Central, Sierra de Neiba, Sierra de Bahoruco

Main Religions   Roman Catholicism, Santeria, Voodoo, Gagá

Major Exports   Ferronickel, sugar, gold, silver, coffee, cocoa, tobacco, meats, consumer goods

Major Imports   Foodstuffs, petroleum, fabrics, chemicals, pharmaceuticals

Trade Partners   United States, Japan, Mexico, Venezuela, Canada, Netherlands, France

Currency   Dominican Peso (34.63 DOP = U.S. $1 as of 2003)

Opposite: **Dominicans enjoy shopping at the farmer's market in Puerto Plata.**

Glossary

Dominican Vocabulary

arroz con leche (ahr-ROHS kohn LEH-cheh): milk and rice pudding.

bachata (bah-CHAH-tah): a folk music.

béisbol (BAYS-bohl): baseball.

carabiné (kah-rah-bee-NEH): a popular Spanish folk dance.

caudillos (kaw-DEE-yohs): military leaders.

cocido (koh-THEE-doh): Spanish stew.

compadrazgo (kohm-pah-DRAS-goh): a godparent relationship.

compadre (kohm-PAD-reh): godparent.

cordillera (kohr-dee-YEH-rah): a mountain range.

criollismo (kree-o-YEES-moh): literature focusing on the lifestyles of Dominicans.

dulce de leche cortada (DOOL-cheh deh LEH-cheh kohr-TAH-dah): sour milk cream similar to yogurt.

encomienda (ehn-koh-mee-EHN-dah): a legal system that gave Spaniards the right to enslave the natives of the countries they conquered.

fritos de batata (FREE-tohs deh bah-TAH-tah): fried sweet potatoes.

fritos maduros (FREE-tohs mah-DOO-rohs): fried ripe plantains.

gallera (gah-YEH-rah): cockfight arena.

gallero (gah-YEH-roh): cockfight handler.

indigenismo (in-dih-heh-NEES-moh): literature that exposed Spanish brutalities toward the Taino.

la bandera (lah bahn-DEH-rah): a dish that consists of white rice, red beans, and fried green plantains.

mangu (mahn-GOO): pureed cassava.

marianismo (mah-ree-ah-NEES-moh): a cultural concept stressing that a woman should liken herself in attitude and everyday living to the Virgin Mary.

pastelito (pahs-teh-LEE-toh): a turnover filled with meat.

platanitos (plah-tah-NEE-tohs): green plantain chips.

postumismo (pohs-tu-MEES-moh): a modern Dominican literary style.

quipes (KEE-pehs): fried cracked wheat and ground beef.

sancocho (sahn-KOH-choh): a meat and vegetable stew.

sarandunga (sah-rahn-DOONG-gah): a Dominican folk dance.

tambora (tahm-BOH-rah): a traditional two-sided drum that can be hit on either side with the hand or a stick.

yaniqueques (jah-nih-KEH-kehs): cornmeal cakes; a type of snack.

English Vocabulary

bicameral: having two separate and distinct lawmaking assemblies.

constitution: the basic laws or principles by which a country is governed.

conquistador: a Spanish conqueror or adventurer in the sixteenth century.

coup: the sudden overthrow of a government and seizure of political power, especially in a violent way.

dictator: a leader who rules a country with absolute power, usually by force.

discrimination: unfair treatment of one person or group usually because of prejudice about a race, ethnic group, religion, or gender.

dissidents: people who are opposed to the views and actions of a society's ruling political party or authority.

ecotourism: tourism in natural settings that involves protecting the environment and causing the least amount of damage or change to those settings.

endangered species: a type of animal, plant, or other organism whose numbers are so few or declining so quickly that it may soon become extinct.

exile: unwilling absence from one's own country; official expulsion from a home country as a punishment.

fluctuated: changed often from high to low levels or from one state of being to another in an unpredictable way.

gross domestic product: the total value of goods produced by a nation in one year.

human encroachment: the gradual movement into and takeover of animal habitats by humans.

ideology: a closely organized system of beliefs, values, and ideas forming the basis of a social, economic, or political philosophy or program.

immigrant: somebody who has come to a country and settled there.

indigenous: original or native; describing the people who occupy a region at the time of its contact with colonial powers.

intervene: to get involved in an event to change what is happening, especially to prevent an undesirable outcome.

manatee: a large, plant-eating mammal found in warm Atlantic coastal waters. It has front flippers and a flattened tail.

merengue: a ballroom dance characterized by a shuffling step; a piece of music for the merengue dance.

montane forests: forests that grow in a relatively cool, humid climate on mountain slopes and contain large evergreen trees.

municipality: a city, town, or other region that has its own local government.

nationalism: patriotism; devotion and loyalty to one's own nation.

occupation: the invasion and control of a country or area by enemy forces.

perpetuated: made something continue, usually for a very long time.

plantains: starchy, greenish fruit resembling a banana.

propaganda: information or ideas spread specifically to promote a cause, movement, or nation.

remittance: money sent by an immigrant to relatives in his or her country of origin.

salvage: the rescue of a ship, its cargo, or crew from loss at sea.

sanitize: to clean; to make something more acceptable by removing anything that might be considered offensive or controversial.

solenodon: a rare nocturnal insect-eating mammal native to the West Indies with a long snout and a long scaly tail. It looks like a large shrew.

unprecedented: having no earlier parallel or equal.

uprising: an act of rebellion or revolt against an authority.

More Books to Read

Christopher Columbus: Explorer. Spirit of America: Our People series. Judy Alter (Child's World)

Dominican Republic in Pictures. Nathan A. Haverstock (Lerner)

Dominican Republic. Major World Nations series. Alexander Creed (Chelsea House)

In the Time of the Butterflies. Julia Alvarez (Dutton/Plume)

Merengue: Dominican Music and Dominican Identity. Paul Austerlitz and Robert Farris Thompson (Temple University Press)

On the Field with...Alex Rodriguez. Matt Christopher (Little, Brown Children's Books)

Pedro Martinez Throwing Strikes. Michael Shalin, Rob Rains (Econo-Clad Books)

Sports Great Sammy Sosa. John Albert Torres (Enslow)

The Color of My Words. Lynn Joseph (HarperCollins Children's Books)

The Dominican Republic. Enchantment of the World second series. Barbara Radcliffe Rogers and Lura Rogers (Children's Book Press)

Videos

Caribbean Close-Up: Haiti & the Dominican Republic. (Library Video)

Dominican Republic. (Tapeworm)

Web Sites

www.dominicanrepublic.com/

lcweb2.loc.gov/frd/cs/dotoc.html

dominicanrepinfo.com/index.htm

www.hispaniola.com/DR/Guides/History.html

www.odci.gov/cia/publications/factbook/geos/dr.html#Govt

Due to the dynamic nature of the Internet, some web sites stay current longer than others. To find additional web sites, use a reliable search engine with one or more of the following keywords to help you locate information about the Dominican Republic. Keywords: *Haiti, Hispaniola, merengue, Pico Duarte, Rafael Trujillo, Santo Domingo.*

Index